CHOICE AND CONSTRAINT IN A
SWAHILI COMMUNITY

CHOICE AND CONSTRAINT IN A
SWAHILI COMMUNITY

PROPERTY, HIERARCHY, AND
COGNATIC DESCENT ON THE
EAST AFRICAN COAST

Ann Patricia Caplan

Published for

THE INTERNATIONAL AFRICAN INSTITUTE

by

OXFORD UNIVERSITY PRESS

LONDON   NEW YORK   NAIROBI

1975

Oxford University Press, Ely House, London W.1

GLASGOW NEW YORK TORONTO MELBOURNE WELLINGTON
CAPE TOWN IBADAN NAIROBI DAR ES SALAAM LUSAKA ADDIS ABABA
DELHI BOMBAY CALCUTTA MADRAS KARACHI LAHORE DACCA
KUALA LUMPUR SINGAPORE HONG KONG TOKYO

ISBN 0 19 724195 6

© International African Institute 1975

Printed in Great Britain by
Richard Clay (The Chaucer Press), Ltd.,
Bungay, Suffolk

For Bibi Emma

CONTENTS

TABLES

FIGURES

CASES

ACKNOWLEDGEMENTS

Field-work on the Island of Mafia was financed by a Travelling Studentship from the University of London, and by a supplementary grant from the Worshipful Company of Goldsmiths. The University of London also financed the subsequent writing-up period. I am extremely grateful to these two bodies for their assistance.

I am also very much indebted to the Government of the United Republic of Tanzania, first of all for permission to work on Mafia, and secondly for facilitating my work in every possible way. In particular, I should like to thank Mr. Njopeka, who was the Island's Area Commissioner at the time of field-work, and the members of his staff.

During my time in Tanzania, I was attached to the University College, Dar es Salaam, and I wish to express my gratitude to members of the academic and administrative staffs for their helpfulness.

Much practical assistance with problems of accommodation, transport, and other matters was given by many people, in particular Mr. Pyarali Kassam, Mr. H. Stanley, Mr. and Mrs. P. Green, and Mr. and Mrs. D'Sousa. Many others on the Island made my stay pleasant and rewarding, and I should like to express my appreciation to Mzee Jumanne Yusufu, 'Sheikh' Msabah Rashid, Bwana Hamis Makame of Baleni, and Bwana Abedi Mzee of Banja. To my cook and helper Salum Ali 'Yesu' I am more grateful than I can say for his unfailing good humour and good sense.

Most of all, I must thank the people whom this work concerns, the villagers of Minazini. The great kindness and patience of people too numerous to mention made my stay among them a most enriching experience.

Finally, I owe a debt of gratitude to the late Professor Wilfred Whiteley, who not only taught me Swahili, but also made possible a visit to the coast in 1962, and later acted as my supervisor while I carried out field-work; also to my former supervisor Professor Philip Gulliver, for his unfailing interest and much-needed encouragement while I was writing up this material for a University of London Ph.D. thesis. Other members of the Department of Anthropology of the School of Oriental and African Studies made helpful comments on drafts of this book, especially Professor J. Middleton, and Drs. D. Parkin and L. Caplan. None of these people are responsible, however, for any of its shortcomings.

PREFACE

This book is about property and power relations in a Swahili village, Minazini,[1] situated in northern Mafia Island off the southern coast of Tanzania, where I carried out field-work between 1965 and 1967. My initial interest in the East African coast was stimulated while I was a student taking a B.A. course in African Studies at London University. I later chose to carry out field-work in this area because, although much had been written of a general nature about the east coast (cf. Bailey 1965 for bibliography), and several anthropologists had worked there (cf. references to Lienhardt, Middleton, Prins, Tanner, and Wijeyewardene in the bibliography) no monograph had yet appeared in print. Indeed, although other anthropologists have subsequently carried out field research on the coast (cf. Bujra 1968), they still have not published their findings in any detail.

Although the Swahili-speaking peoples of the coastal belt share many cultural features, especially language and religion, and have a broadly similar economy (subsistence agriculture coupled with a certain dependence upon cash from the sale of copra, cashew nuts, and/or cloves), they do not form a 'tribe' in any accepted sense. However, as Wijeyewardene has pointed out, one of their most important distinguishing features is their residence in nucleated, autonomous villages, some of which, at one time, were powerful 'city-states'. One of my aims in writing this book, then, apart from anything else, is to present a detailed study of a single Swahili village, Minazini, in which I spent over a year. 'Village studies' are, after all, fairly unusual in the context of Africa, which has generated mainly 'tribal studies'.

Apart from wishing to study a community in depth, I also wanted when I began field-work to try to make sense of the kinship system, which earlier writings had indicated was quite different from the usual unilineal 'African model'. Soon after I had begun field-work, I realized that not only is there a cognatic kinship system in Mafia, but also that unrestricted cognatic descent *groups* are an important feature of the villages in northern Mafia (although not in the south), and that these groupings have considerable similarity with those reported from Zanzibar and Pemba by Middleton (1961).

I do not propose in this book to present in any detail the arguments for and against calling the types of groups found in northern Mafia (and Zanzibar and Pemba) 'descent groups', since I have already discussed this at some length elsewhere (Caplan 1969). I would however point out that a lack of consensus among anthropologists on the terms for, and exact status of, what in this book I have termed cognatic descent groups has led to a great deal of confusion about Swahili kinship and descent. Some anthropologists who have worked on the coast, notably Lienhardt and Middleton, have also referred to these groups as cognatic (or nonunilineal) descent groups. But others have not viewed them in this way. Tanner, working in the Tanga region, refers to unilineal lineages (perhaps a reflection of the preoccupations of anthropology at the time he carried out his work), while Wijeyewardene refers to the groupings in his two Swahili villages as 'kindreds', following the example set by Leach in *Pul Eliya*; both Leach and Wijeyewardene in fact, refuse to accept the existence of any descent groups other than unilineal ones.

It does seem likely however, that cognatic descent groups are an important feature of many parts of coastal society, although not all (for example they do not exist in southern Mafia, or in Pate in northern Kenya, cf. Bujra 1968), but that their size and relative importance in the social structure varies considerably from one part of the coast to another.

Since my field-work was carried out, more data on societies with similar kinship and descent systems has appeared, notably Scheffler's study of Choiseul Island (1965, 1966), a number of articles by Keesing concerning the Kwaio (in particular 1967a, 1967b, 1970), and a study by Hanson of the Rapa (1970a, 1970b); all of these works describe cognatic descent among Oceanic peoples. Scheffler's book is basically a reconstruction of a society as it existed at the turn of the century, rather than of one which was functioning at the time of field-work, and this is also true of information on kinship and descent given in Hanson's work. And although Keesing describes Kwaio society as having a 'cognatic ideology', it is plain that this takes second place to a much stronger agnatic ideology.

New material regarding non-unilineal descent has also been forthcoming from Africa, and this would seem to indicate that anthropologists working there are finally beginning to realize that 'African models' are not necessarily synonymous with unilineal ones. Good examples of this line of thinking are provided by Lloyd's work on the Yoruba (1966) and Gulliver's study of the Ndendeuli (1971). Another important recent book on cognatic kinship and descent is Bloch's study of the Merina of Madagascar (1971). However in neither Merina nor Ndendeuli society does a cognatic descent *ideology* go along with cognatic descent *groups*, as in northern Mafia.

A study of land tenure among the Amhara of Ethiopia (Hoben 1973) reveals that cognatic descent groups do exist in that society, and indeed, that study constitutes the first monograph dealing with an African society which has such descent groups. However, among the Amhara, descent groups are not multipurpose, as on Mafia Island; their sole function is the control of land, and the way in which they do this is very different to the control exercised by the Mafia descent groups.

In view of the dearth of ethnographic information on societies in Africa, or indeed elsewhere in the world where such descent groups are to be found, inevitably one of the main purposes of this book is to show how such groups actually work 'on the ground', and how the 'problem' of choice of membership raised by Leach (1962) and others is resolved.

However, although the focus is on the workings of the descent groups, I do not seek to present them as *the* basic structural units of society, but rather as one among a number of frameworks (or conscious models, or idioms) which are used by the people themselves to talk about their society, and which are also useful to the anthropologist in making an analysis. Thus the personal network (*jamaa*) constitutes a second conscious model, and the socio-religious hierarchy found on the Island a third. Each of these has its own norms, which provide constraints on choice, but together they form a dynamic system which leaves the individual with a wide range of options in any given situation.

In seeking to show how the cognatic descent groups in Minazini village actually operate, I present both an ideology of descent group membership and also numerical material about how people affiliate in those contexts in which the descent groups are significant. The reason why people choose to affiliate (i.e. activate their membership) as they do is a complex issue in a society where, because membership of groups is overlapping, choice is 'built in' to the system. Like others who have written on cognatic descent systems, I have found it necessary to discuss in some detail the constraints governing choices, and thereby to construct not only mechanical and statistical models, but also to employ a third kind of model, which has been variously termed a 'decision model' (Keesing 1967a), an 'action model' (Ogan 1966) and a 'self-interest model' (Scheffler 1965).

The first Chapter of the book provides the necessary background to the study. It gives first a brief history of Mafia Island, and then an outline of the population categories found there today. This is followed by a description of Minazini village and its economy.

The second Chapter presents the structure of the descent groups and shows how this is affected by the high rate of kin marriage. This chapter also introduces another important framework, that of the *jamaa* (personal network) which both cuts across and extends beyond the descent groups. The norm of kin marriage (i.e. marriage within the *jamaa*) affects the structure of the descent groups; indeed, it can be argued that, given a system of cognatic descent groups which is unrestricted by such factors as residence, a reasonably high rate of group endogamy must take place, or else, within a few generations, everyone would be a member of every group (cf. Hanson 1970b).

The third and fourth Chapters are both concerned with land-holding; the former with residential rights, and the latter with rights to cultivable land. In this context, the descent groups are seen to be units of the same order—each is a corporate entity in respect of the land which it holds, although in actual fact some groups hold more land in relation to their size than do others. The factors which affect individual decisions about where to live and cultivate are diverse, and include a consideration not only of descent group membership, but also of ownership of coconut trees, the developmental cycle of households and household clusters, frequency of divorce, and the practice of fostering children; the degree of involvement in various kinds of ritual and political activities is also an important element in decisions about land-usage.

The second part of the book—Chapters five to seven—is concerned mainly with the relationship between the descent groups and the socio-religious hierarchy in the village. Here, the groups are not of the same order. First of all, status is not held by descent groups in quite the same way as is land; certain members of certain groups have high status, and certain members of other groups have low status. In this way, the groups themselves come to be ranked in the hierarchy. Through manipulation of their descent group affiliation, and through their adherence to what is viewed in Minazini as the most orthodox forms of Islam, a small number of people, mostly members of a single descent group, are able to claim high socio-religious status; because they are accorded this status, they are able to control not only most of the Islamic institutions in the village, but also political offices too. Power of a different kind is wielded by the members of another descent group, who control spirit possession guilds, and hence important weapons in the battle against disease and death. Such people are, however, accorded low socio-religious status, and until recently have been excluded from the main loci of power in the village, that is, the Friday mosque and the Village Development Committee.

The question of choice in a situation where many individuals belong to more than one group is discussed again in detail in the final chapter; here choice of affiliation to descent groups in a number of contexts —marriage, residence, land-holding, Islamic activities, and spirit possession—is compared. Some descent groups, namely those associated with a particular resource, such as land or political power, are shown to be more 'corporate' than others, that is, a relatively high proportion of their members affiliate with them in these contexts, while other groups which control fewer resources attract fewer of their members.

In this final chapter, too, the relationship between the three types of models used in this book is discussed again, and it is suggested that it is the combination of mechanical, statistical, and decision models which provides us with as full an explanation of Minazini society as possible.

A.P.C.
July 1974

CHAPTER 1

ECOLOGY, POPULATION, AND ECONOMY

Mafia is a large island lying off the southern coast of Tanzania, near to the Rufiji Delta. It is 30 miles long (from north to south), and up to 10 miles in width; its total area is nearly 200 square miles, which is rather more than half the area of Zanzibar Island further to the north. Like Zanzibar, Mafia is a raised portion of the continental shelf, not a coral island. The soil of Mafia is mostly sandy and the terrain very flat. There is a ridge forming a backbone to the northern end, but at its highest point it does not exceed 200 feet above sea level. Along this ridge, there is firm and fertile clay soil, and cultivation of annual crops is possible. On the eastern shores there is some coral rock; here nothing can be grown, and there is no habitation.

The climate of Mafia is typically coastal, except that it has an annual rainfall of 76 inches, which is somewhat higher than on the mainland. Most of the rain falls between March and June. There tends to be rather less rain in the north of the island, where trees are fewer. It has been suggested that the densely planted coconut trees in the south act as a kind of 'rain forest'; they also make it somewhat cooler in the south. The temperature is usually around 80° F for most of the year, and rarely rises above 90° in the hot season between December and March.

History and population of Mafia Island

Mafia has a heterogeneous population, reflecting its chequered history.[1] The island appears never to have produced an independent culture. In mediaeval times it was known only as an appendage of Kilwa,[2] and later it came under the rule of the Busaidi Sultans in Zanzibar. In 1890, during the colonial period, Mafia became a part of German East Africa, i.e. Tanganyika. During World War I British troops took control, and Mafia subsequently became a part of the

League of Nations Trustee Territory of Tanganyika. Since 1964 it has constituted part of the United Republic of Tanzania which was formed by the union of Tanganyika and Zanzibar after the revolution in the latter island.

While Zanzibar was ruling Mafia in the nineteenth century, many Arabs settled, acquired land, and planted coconut trees which are more suited to the sandy soil of Mafia than the cloves which the Arabs cultivated in Zanzibar. The Arabs ran their plantations with slave labour imported from the African mainland. As the Arabs planted more and more trees in the southern half of Mafia, the original inhabitants of the Island, the Mbwera,[3] were pushed farther north.

Later, Germans and British established large plantations in the south. These became more prosperous than the Arab plantations which fell into decline after the freeing of the slaves in 1922. Many Arabs mortgaged their land to Indians, who had come to the Island later in the nineteenth century, or else sold it outright. Whereas in 1911 it was estimated that the Arabs owned over 60 per cent of all the trees on the Island, by 1935 they owned only 30 per cent.[4] It is likely that they own an even smaller proportion of the trees now, although no recent figures are available.

According to the 1967 census there is a total population of 16,748 persons on the Island, giving a density of 83·7 persons per square mile. The majority of the population are Africans, among whom three sub-categories may be discerned. Firstly there are 'free born' (*Waungwana*) Africans, called Mbwera, who were settled on Mafia before the Arabs came; these do not form a tribe in any of the usually accepted senses. They probably crossed over from the mainland[5] over a long period of time. Their highest concentration is in the northern part of the island; few are to be found south of Baleni village (see Fig. 1). They identify themselves with the Shirazii who are found all along the coast and claim to be the descendants of Persian immigrants who came to the coast in the tenth century A.D. (cf. Bailey 1965: 119–22 for further details).

Apart from the Mbwera or Shirazii there are also people calling themselves Pokomo who claim to have come to Mafia more recently than the Mbwera. Some of them say that they were brought to the Island by the Portuguese from their original home on the Kenya coast. Pokomo are only to be found in the northern villages of the Island.

Secondly, there are Africans of slave descent (*watumwa*). There are relatively few of these in the north of the Island, but south of Baleni village, they constitute a large proportion of the population. Unfortunately it is not possible to obtain figures of their numbers as in the census charts they, like the Mbwera and Pokomo, are subsumed under the general heading of 'Africans'. Very few of them will admit

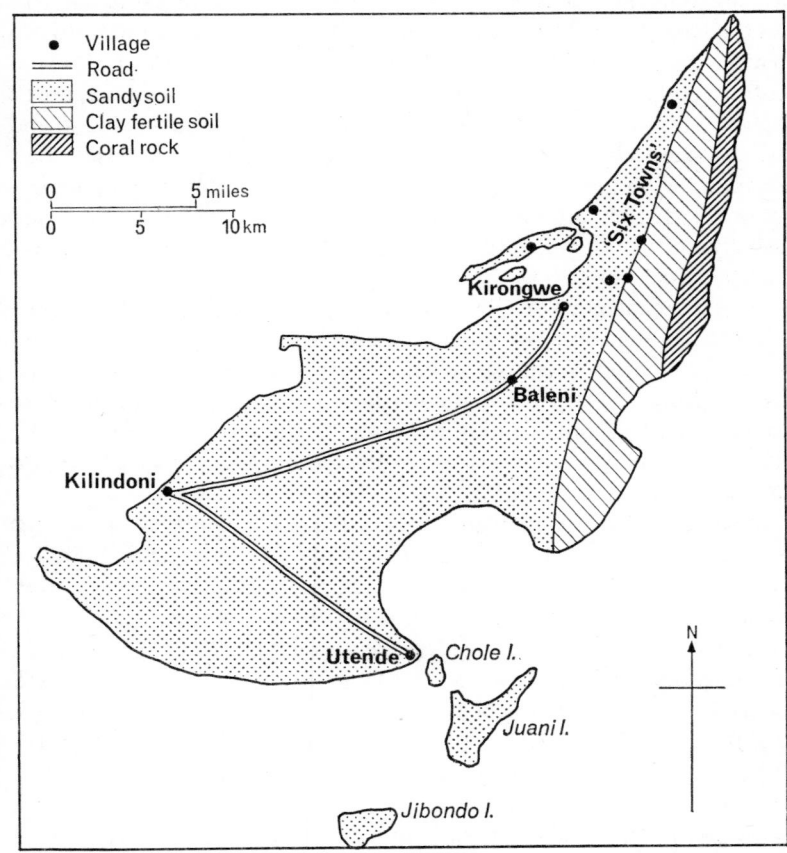

FIG. I

Mafia Island

to being of slave descent, as this means admitting that they are inferior to the 'free born', although they sometimes refer to themselves as being members of inland tribes, e.g. Nyasa, Zaramo. Women of slave descent have been married by Mbwera and Pokomo and also by Arabs, but it is still very rare for a male of ex-slave status to marry a 'free born' woman. However, the descendants of slaves live side by side with the Mbwera and Pokomo and it is often difficult to distinguish them. All are Muslims, and speak the same dialect of Swahili.

The third category is composed of mainland Africans, from areas inland from the coast, most of whom are recent immigrants working on the large Indian- and European-owned plantations in the southern part of the Island. Many have been assimilated into the local Muslim culture and have taken local wives. However they are often regarded by the Mbwera as being of only slightly superior status to slaves, and are unlikely to marry 'free born' women. There are also other immigrants, notably Makonde from Mozambique who are totally un-assimilated; they are Christians who dress in 'western' fashion, and usually speak poor Swahili. They are despised by the Muslim inhabitants of the Island.

The final category of Africans, immigrants from other parts of the coast, such as people from Kilwa, Zanzibar, Pemba, and Lamu, and from the Comoro Islands, are easily absorbed by the Mbwera, who treat them as equals, or even superiors. This particularly applies to the immigrants from Lamu, the Bajuni, locally known as Gunya, who have traditionally claimed Arab status, although other Mafian Arabs do not recognize this claim.

In addition to the Africans there are a small minority of Indians and Arabs. Most of the former live in the administrative capital of Kilindoni. They run the twenty or so shops there, and engage in other business, including running two large coconut plantations.

Arabs constitute a category less easy to define. Most Mafia Arabs are descended from male immigrants who married African wives, and many of them are physically indistinguishable from Africans. The majority of long-established Arabs call themselves Shatiri or El-Kanaan, and there are in addition a few more recent immigrants who retain contact with their homeland (e.g. Hadhramaut) and whose first language is still Arabic rather than Swahili. The Arabs have always constituted an élite on the coast. They have been the wealthiest people, the most assiduous in orthodox Islamic observance, and have had the most political power. Since the culture of the coast has traditionally been 'Arab-oriented', it is a matter of prestige to be as much like an Arab as possible in dress, speech, and manners (cf. Caplan 1974).

However, changing circumstances since independence have altered matters somewhat, and this is reflected in the number of people on Mafia as elsewhere on the coast, claiming Arab status. At the time of the 1957 census, prior to independence, there were 663 people on Mafia claiming to be Arabs, but this number had dropped considerably by the time of the 1967 census.[6]

The economy of the Island

The south of the Island, as I have already suggested, is much richer than the north. The soil in the south is sandy, and peculiarly suited to the growing of coconut trees. For this reason, the majority of Arabs settled there, and established their plantations. With the growth of the plantation economy, a network of roads was constructed. In addition, the administrative capital always lay in the south. Under the Germans the capital was at Chole Island; later it was moved to its present site at Kilindoni.

Under German rule it was compulsory for every able-bodied male to plant at least 50 coconut trees. This pressure, combined with the growth of the copra trade and a need for cash to pay taxes, forced even the Mbwera and Pokomo in the north, previously dependent upon rice and other annual crops, cattle, and fishing, to begin to plant trees. Nevertheless there is still plenty of spare land in the northern areas, but very little in the south where it has all been planted with trees. Generally people in the south depend more upon cash income from copra and cashew nuts for their livelihood; in the north they are dependent primarily upon cultivation of annual crops.

For the last fifty years at least copra has provided the principal means of obtaining cash for the majority of Mafians. Recently, however, with a slump in world copra prices, cashew nuts have assumed greater importance, and the production of nuts has increased fourfold in the sixties, to 1,124 tons in 1966. This is still only about a third of the copra tonnage, but the cashew nuts fetch a higher price (1s. per kilo)[7] than do coconuts (70 cents per kilo). Cashew nut trees flourish on sandy soil; they are thus mainly found in the south, and only a few grow north of Kirongwe village.

Apart from the cultivation of these two cash crops opportunities for obtaining a cash income are very limited. Educationally the Mafians are very backward, with only a handful of children receiving a secondary education on the mainland.[8] However, a few of the children who have attended local primary schools and then failed to get one of the few places available in a secondary school have been absorbed into government service in Mafia.

It is only in the south of the Island that a few men have been able to improve their economic status by becoming drivers or owners of vehicles for transporting cash crops to the collecting centres. Indeed, it is only in the south that there are any motorable roads; in the north people transport their goods by donkey. In the south too are to be found all the large dhows (*majahazi*) which carry goods and passengers between Mafia and the mainland. In the north, by contrast, there are only a handful of the smaller type of dhow (*mashua*).

Apart from the growing of cash crops, fishing is the most important source of income for the majority of people. Much of the fish is sold in the markets at Kirongwe and Kilindoni and some is exported to Dar es Salaam. Unfortunately it is impossible to give figures for the total exports of fish from the Island, as no records are kept.

In giving this brief background to the history, population, and economy of the Island, I have emphasized the differences between the north and south—primarily that in the south the population is more heterogeneous, and the economy more diverse and advanced than in the north. In addition there are striking differences in settlement patterns; northern villages are discrete units, unlike the villages in the south which are dispersed settlements and can hardly be called villages at all except in an administrative sense. The north may be said to begin after Kirongwe, and indeed the northerners themselves frequently refer to their villages as the Six Towns (*Miji Sita*).

Minazini village: Population

The village which is the focus of this study is situated in the north of Mafia, and is one of the largest communities on the Island, with a total population of nearly 1,000 people. As in the other northern villages, many of the houses are grouped together around a focal point. In the case of Minazini, this is formed by the three shops, the dispensary, and the TANU [9] office. But further away from this centre the houses are spread out among the coconut trees.

Most houses are built of a framework of mangrove poles filled in with mud and thatched with coconut palm fronds. They usually consist of several rooms and an open verandah at the front, where the men gather to talk; women work and receive their friends in an enclosed courtyard at the back of the house. Some houses, generally belonging to younger people, are built only of plaited palm fronds (*makuti*).

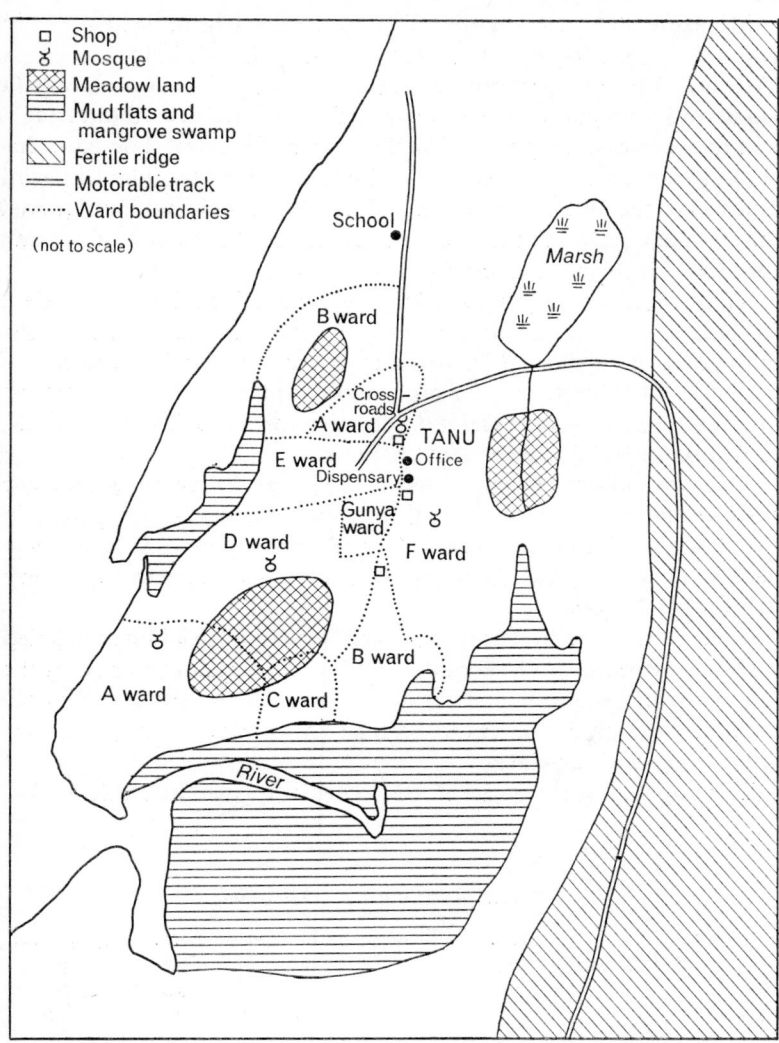

Shop
Mosque
Meadow land
Mud flats and
  mangrove swamp
Fertile ridge
Motorable track
Ward boundaries
(not to scale)

School

Marsh

B ward

Cross-
roads
A ward

TANU
Office

E ward

Dispensary

Gunya
ward

F ward

D ward

A ward

B ward

C ward

River

FIG. 2
Minazini Village

Minazini, like other northern villages, is fairly homogeneous in population, and most of the villagers may be broadly classed as 'African'. The only exceptions are the members of an Arab family (a Hadhrami immigrant, his wife, whose family is from southern Mafia, and their six children) and a small number of Gunya. The latter include a brother and a sister who claim Sharif[10] status. The Minazini Gunya are the children or grandchildren of the original immigrants, but, unlike Gunya in other parts of Mafia, they have not retained any contact with their homeland in northern Kenya.

The 'Africans' in the village may be divided into three categories: Mbwera, Pokomo, and descendants of slaves. There are also a few immigrants from the mainland and from other parts of the coast. The categories of Mbwera and Pokomo are not exclusive as they are much intermarried and people claim different status on different occasions, as will be shown in subsequent chapters.

The descendants of slaves[11] form a single exclusive category, since ex-slave status is inherited only through the father. Twenty people in the village fall into this category. There are many more villagers who had slave mothers, but this does not affect their status as 'free born' Mbwera or Pokomo.

Finally, the immigrants: those from the coast have all inter-married with the Mbwera and Pokomo. A handful who claim to be from the Zaramo tribe (whose homeland is just north of the Rufiji Delta) are thought privately by others to be really of ex-slave status, and they inter-marry with ex-slaves.

The population categories in the village are given in Table 1.

TABLE I
Population categories in Minazini

Category	Men	Women	Children	Total	% of total
Mbwera & Pokomo	189	260	420	869	93·4
Gunya	6	4	6	16	1·7
Ex-slaves	9	6	5	20	2·0
Zaramo	2	2	7	11	1·0
Arabs	1	1	6	8	0·8
Other mainlanders	2	1	0	3	0·3
Other coastal (Z'bar etc.)	1	2	0	3	0·3
Total	210	276	444	930	99·5

Economy of the village

AGRICULTURE

The economy of Minazini village is based on rice and cassava cultivation, with coconuts as the main cash crop. Cattle keeping, fishing, and trading provide secondary sources of income. The most important food crop grown in the village is rice. This is cultivated on two types of land: wet meadow land within the village (*dawe*), which can be cultivated for a number of years in succession, and bush land (*pori*), which lies in a belt around the village, and is under shifting cultivation.

The agricultural season begins in early November, when the men cut down and fire the bush. The women then plant rice in December. Planting begins a little later on the wet lands, and since it is only necessary to weed the ground before planting, women can, and frequently do cultivate this type of land alone. Planting methods are extremely simple, as indeed are all the agricultural techniques in this area. Small hand-hoes are used which only scratch the surface of the soil.

As soon as the rice begins to sprout, in January or February, a constant watch has to be kept on the fields in order to ensure that the entire crop is not lost to birds, monkeys, pigs, and hippopotamus. Women and children spend all day in the fields, often sitting in small wooden watch towers, and scaring off the smaller pests with slings and stones. The men meanwhile build fences to encircle the fields; these are generally built around a whole cultivated area, which includes several fields, and the men in any one area work together to build the fence. In February, people who are cultivating a bush field, and some of those cultivating a wet field, move out to small huts they have built among their crops, leaving their houses in the village. Some people stay as long as five months in the fields, from the first sprouting of the rice until it has all been harvested. In spite of all these efforts, however, much of the crop is lost.

As would be expected with such a simple technology, the yield is small, although, since land is not held on an individual basis (cf. Chapter 4), acreages vary considerably according to factors such as age, marital status, and sheer capacity for hard work. On average, a young couple can cultivate around $2\frac{1}{2}$–3 acres of bush land or $2\frac{1}{4}$ acres of wet land. Older women cultivating alone manage only $\frac{1}{4}$–$\frac{1}{2}$ acre of bush land, or slightly more wet land. Other factors which affect yields include rainfall, incidence of pests (birds, animals, and insects), and the type of land being cultivated. Wet land produces more rice per acre than bush, but only rice can be grown there. Bush land, on the other hand, also produces corn, millet, beans, etc., and some bush land which is very stony, and produces a poor crop of rice, does yield sesame, which may be sold and the proceeds used to buy rice or other foods.

The second staple is cassava, which is grown mainly in an area of bush set aside for this purpose by the Government Agricultural Officer. Most men have a cassava as well as a rice field. Cassava has the advantage of being a hardy crop, needing little attention once it is planted, and villagers do not need to guard cassava fields. Another important food is sweet potatoes, which are grown in the wet fields after the rice has been harvested. Potatoes form a substantial part of the diet in July, August, and September.

Most people thus have a fairly varied diet. In January those cultivating bush fields live on beans, which is the first crop to be harvested. By March everyone is eating rice and pumpkins. Much rice is consumed between March and May, when the villagers return to their houses. After May people eat the remainder of their rice, and any other crop they may have grown such as corn. In addition they eat cassava, and those families which have a good harvest are able to vary their diet by eating cassava at mid-day and rice in the evening. In this way some people manage to make their rice supplies last until October. But rice is considered the best kind of food, and is always used for feasts, so that those people who have to give a feast themselves, or contribute to that of a relative, will find that most of their rice is finished by September.

The main point to be noted is that few people produce sufficient food for their needs. By September the village shops are selling flour, rice, and beans, mostly imported from the mainland via Kilindoni and Kirongwe, and continue to do so until January or February. On the whole, then, most people produce only enough for 7–8 months of the year; staple food for the remaining 4–5 months has to be bought.

Other foods are bought daily all the year round—these include sugar, tea and cakes (*mandazi*) made of rice flour which are eaten for breakfast by those households which can afford them. Then, unless there is a fisherman in the household, fish has to be purchased daily (chicken and meat are eaten only at feasts). In addition most men smoke, and cigarettes are bought in the village shops.

Thus the average daily cash needs for a nuclear family of husband, wife, and two children (in fact the size of the average household is 3·5 persons—cf. Chapter 3) would be a minimum of 1s. during the period when they are eating their own produce, and about three times that amount during the 'hungry months' when the harvest has finished.

Apart from daily needs money is also spent during the year on clothes (ideally one new set per person) and on taxes (30s. per annum for each adult male), school fees for children,[12] and licences for radios (3 in the village), for bicycles (2 of these), and for shops (as already mentioned, 3 in number). Annual cash needs may thus be shown as follows:—

TABLE 2
Annual cash needs

	Man	Woman	Child
Clothes	80s.	110s.	45s.
Taxes and school fees	30s.	—	10s.
Food	390s.	140s.*	55s.
Total expenditure	500s.	250s.	110s.

Note: * The figure is much lower for a woman, because some items are bought for the household as a whole, e.g. sugar, tea, fish, and are thus entered in the husband's column. Households of which women are the head, however, would have a larger amount of expenditure in the woman's column.

Sources of cash income—internal

(a) COCONUT TREES

The most important source of cash income is copra, but the exact amount usually derived from its sale in a normal year is difficult to estimate, because the years during which the study was made were also years in which the income was unusually small. Two factors account for this. The first was the fall in the price of copra, and the general difficulties of marketing, due to the teething troubles at the inception of the Co-operatives.[13] The second factor was the poor rainfall in 1965 and 1966; only 45 inches of rain fell in the latter year, and even less in the former, compared with a normal annual average of 76 inches.

In a normal year a person owning 100 coconut trees could expect to fell 4,000 nuts, giving a gross income of 800s., and a net income of around 620s.[14] However, in 1966, with the drop in yields, only 2,750 nuts could be sold, and at a lower price, giving a gross income of only 385s., or 200s. net profit.[15] This obviously represents a considerable drop in income. Table 3 shows the distribution of coconut trees and the income to be derived from them among the population of the village:

TABLE 3
Ownership of coconut trees and income per annum

Number of trees	0	1–50	50–100	100–200	200–500	500+
Net income p.a.	—	0–100s.	100–200s.	200–400s.	400–1000s.	1000s.+
(1966)						
Male owners	53	43	44	35	16	3
Female owners	170	76	15	11	2	0
All owners	223	119	59	46	18	3

Note: These figures are based on my own observations of yields, where possible, and information given by villagers. However, they are only approximate, as yields tend to fluctuate somewhat according to area, age of tree, etc.

Coconut trees are acquired by inheritance, buying, and planting. Since men inherit twice as much as women under Islamic law, and also have greater opportunities for acquiring cash with which to buy trees, they generally own more trees than women. Indeed, the average per male owner is 125 trees, whereas the average per woman owner is only 36 trees, and a substantially higher number of women than men own no trees at all. Furthermore, most trees are owned by older men, not only because they have already received their inheritance but also because they will probably at some point in their lives have planted trees or managed to acquire some by buying.

(b) ANIMALS

Another potential source of income in Minazini is cattle, of which there are 450 head in the village. They are distributed among 117 owners, giving an average of just under four cattle per owner. However, two men, both spirit shamans, own more than 50 head each, so that if they are omitted from the reckoning the average number per owner is three.

The cattle produce very little milk, perhaps half a pint a day in the short wet season. Their chief value is as a source of meat. Cattle are sold to be slaughtered at marriages, puberty ceremonies, funerals, spirit possession dances, and certain Islamic rituals. On average, one animal per fortnight is slaughtered in the village for these purposes. It is rare for a man to slaughter a beast just to sell the meat, as this brings in very little money and is resorted to only when an animal has injured itself. Selling an animal for a feast, however, fetches between 150s. and 250s. in cash.

Cattle are herded by men who do this work almost full time, and usually look after the animals of several owners. They are paid an agreed proportion of the calves born, and also dispose of the milk. Herding cattle is considered to be rather a menial occupation, fit only for youths and the simple-minded.

There are also a number of donkeys in the village. Unlike cattle, donkeys are usually looked after by their owners, who also take them to Kirongwe carrying copra and returning with goods for the village shops. A donkey owner can make 6s.–10s. on a single trip, which takes up to half a day; donkeys are thus more profitable than cattle, and they sell for a minimum of 300s.

There are also a few goats in the village which are occasionally slaughtered at small feasts, and in connection with a certain type of spirit possession ritual. They fetch between 80s. and 100s.

(c) FISHING

Although there are no large dhows (*majahazi* or *mashua*) which can be used by teams of fishermen, many Minazini fishermen do own outrigger canoes (*ngalawa*) which are useful for fishing just offshore. Some 79 men, or 38 per cent of the male adult population, are regularly engaged in fishing in some form. The most profitable type of fishing is that done with large traps (*wando*), which require a team of four or five men, and can net up to 2,000 fish at a single tide. The season during which these can be used is however rather short, lasting only about six months, and a trap can rarely be used again after the end of a season. They are extremely expensive to buy, costing around 600s. each, and at the start of the 1966 fishing season only two Minazini men had managed to raise the necessary capital. However, the profits are relatively large, around 9–1200s. in a season, and are shared between the trap owner, who receives half, and his team, who share the remainder equally between themselves. The fish are dried or smoked by the fishing team, and are then sold to village traders, who take them to sell in Dar es Salaam.

Other men fish on a somewhat smaller scale with nets (*nailoni* or *nyavu*). There were three large nets operating in the village in 1966, all bought with loans (see below) and worked by teams of two or three men. Other men own small nets which they use themselves. Sometimes the large nets bring in sufficient fish to sell to the traders, but most of the fish caught in this way are sold in the village.

Finally, other men fish alone with basket traps or lines, but they rarely catch even enough to sell; they generally consume whatever they obtain themselves.

(d) TRADE

Trading provides another important source of cash income. Some 48 men (23 per cent of the adult males) travel regularly to Dar es Salaam to sell fish, mats, and chickens, or to Zanzibar to sell dried grass (*ukindu*) used in the making of mats. Most traders do not make large profits, but a handful have succeeded in improving their economic status by this means, and have made trading almost a full-time occupation. Apart from regular traders, most men in the village at some time in their lives are able to raise the capital to buy a stock of goods and make a trading trip with them; this is a means of 'seeing the world' of Dar es Salaam and Zanzibar. Traders return to the village with a miscellaneous selection of goods including dates, salt, clothes, and jewellery.

There are three shops in Minazini, two owned by villagers and the third belonging to an Arab who formerly resided there but subsequently moved to Kirongwe. The shops stock a small range of goods—flour, tea, sugar, beans, kerosene, soap, and a few items like combs, exercise books, and mirrors. Nearly all of these goods are obtained from the shops in Kirongwe, thus making the profit margin very slight, and raising the price of the goods, which have already passed through the hands of middlemen in Dar es Salaam and Kilindoni, as well as Kirongwe, and also incurred considerable transportation costs. Even so, the total profits are high enough to make the shop-keepers among the wealthier persons in the village.

(e) OTHER INTERNAL INCOME SOURCES

As I have said, there is little opportunity for people to earn money outside the village, as there is no job market even in the south of the Island. Within the village some younger men make a little money by acting as coconut fellers or breakers of nuts; occasionally there is a demand for porters to carry goods from the village to the shore, or to and from Kirongwe.

A few men earn money because of special skills—one man is a carpenter, and there are several tailors. A handful of people receive a government salary, including the VEO (Village Executive Officer) and TANU secretary (cf. Chapter 7), the dresser and his assistant at the dispensary, and the three school-teachers who live at the school itself, situated half-way between Minazini and a neighbouring village. At the time of study only the VEO and the dresser's assistant were local men; the rest were posted from southern Mafia (the latter are not included in my census, as they were not always resident in the village, and also did not participate at all in village affairs).

Each year between 20 and 30 men from the village are employed by the administration for a few weeks to repair the dry-weather motorable track which runs from Kirongwe to the northernmost village of the Island. Priority is given to those men who have not paid their taxes.

Cash is also earned within the village by ritual specialists, who include such people as Koranic teachers (*walim*, sing. *mwalim*) and spirit shamans (*waganga*, sing. *mganga*), to be discussed in greater detail in the latter half of this book. Three of the *walim* in the village hold Koranic classes for children; others confine their activities to divination by astrology, and preparing amulets and charms (*hirizi*). None of these activities brings in a particularly large income, although they do carry considerable prestige. It is usually men from the upper income brackets who are able to afford the time to become *walim*.

Spirit shamans on the other hand may come from any economic category. They work as diviners, and also use their knowledge of herbs and influence with spirits to cure physical and mental sickness. Successful *waganga* can become wealthy men by local standards, but the majority do not earn a large income from their activities.

It may be noted that within the village itself, there is no one who lends money on a semi-commercial basis. The shopkeepers give some credit and wealthy men will occasionally lend small sums to close relatives, but on the whole there is very little indebtedness, and no mortgaging.

External income sources

Although opportunities for earning cash in the village are thus very limited, labour migration is not an important factor in the economy, probably because until recently cash from the sale of copra was sufficient to meet needs. A few men from the village have migrated to

Dar es Salaam, and work as petty traders. One of the richest men in Minazini is mostly resident in the capital, where he sells the mats which he buys on his periodic trips back to the village. He invests most of his money in Minazini, mainly in the form of coconut trees, and has also built a fine large house. His wife and children remain in the village, and he himself plans to retire there.

But this man is not typical of migrants. The commonest pattern is for young men aged between 16 and 20 to spend a year or so in Zanzibar Town. They say that they go to 'see the world', and their elders say that they 'have their fling' before returning to marry in the village and settle down to sober lives. Before the Zanzibar revolution some men went annually to pick cloves, but this is no longer possible, and indeed it seems likely that in recent years the number going to Zanzibar has decreased, while more youths are going to Dar es Salaam instead. Very few of these young migrants manage to bring back any money with them; I even heard parents complaining that they had to send them their return fares!

There is however, a minority which stays for longer periods; these men either take their wives with them or else marry local women. Even so, most of them return to the village eventually, because they inherit property there and can always obtain land. In Zanzibar and Dar es Salaam, on the other hand, once they are past working age they rarely have any security. Very few manage to make enough money to build their own houses or buy trees or other forms of capital, and the tiny minority which does succeed in doing this usually remains there permanently.

Emigrants keep in close contact with their relatives by means of the traders who are frequent visitors, and they invariably stay with relatives and fellow-villagers when they first arrive in Zanzibar or Dar es Salaam.

Emigration thus provides an alternative to staying in the village and earning an income by farming or fishing. However, since most of the emigrants work as labourers for very low wages, they eventually return no richer than when they left.

Women and cash earnings

It will be noted that all of the foregoing means of earning cash (with the exception of selling copra) are primarily male-dominated occupations. Women have very few means of obtaining money except by plaiting mats. All women do this, and can expect to earn around 50s.

per annum. A few women also make additional amounts through special skills such as baking cakes, hairdressing, or making clay pots, but the sums involved are very small. Most of them spend money earned in these ways on clothes for themselves or their children. As noted, some women also have an income from their coconut trees, and since, under Islamic law, husbands are obliged to maintain them adequately, this money is in theory theirs to spend as they please. In fact, of course, given the poverty of most households in the village, the wife's income is normally pooled with that of the husband.

New economic opportunities

The main type of new economic opportunity being created in the village is through loans. These were originally made by the District Council, and are now channelled through the Co-operative societies. However, the amount of money available for loans is very limited, and the lenders have to be fairly sure that they will be repaid. Accordingly, the recipients of loans fall into two categories—those who are already wealthy, with capital such as coconut trees or cattle, which could be taken in lieu of repayment, or else holders of political office. Since the latter tend to be in any case among the richer members of the community, the loan system to a large extent maintains the *status quo*. However, it does allow for the employment of other men, e.g. as fishermen in the *wando* teams.

Distribution of wealth in Minazini

Three points may be added to the foregoing discussion. The first is that on the whole wealth is concentrated in the hands of middle-aged or old people. Secondly, men own more property than women, partly because of the 2:1 ratio of inheritance under Islamic law (cf. Chapter 3), and partly because women have far fewer opportunities for making money than men do. The third point is that at the moment, opportunities for economic improvement are extremely limited, and, as far as could be gauged, property tends to remain mostly in the hands of the same people. Only a few people manage to build up wealth through their own efforts, usually through trading or being a spirit shaman, and raise their economic status.

There are, then, considerable differences in the cash incomes of villagers. Over a third of the male population has an annual cash income of less than 250s. while 3 per cent have an income in excess of 2,000s. per annum, as table 4 shows:

TABLE 4
Total cash incomes[16] *(men)*

Income per annum	% of adult male population
0–250s.	37
250s.–500s.	22
500s.–1000s.	25
1000s.–2000s.	13
2000s.–8000s.	3
Total	100

Note: I have based these figures on an assessment of the earnings of labourers, fishermen, traders, and specialists, and also on the annual income from coconut trees, cattle, and donkeys.

Household viability

On the basis of these figures it is now possible to see to what extent people are able to meet their cash needs, which have already been discussed earlier in this chapter. This, of course, depends not only on cash incomes, but also on the size of the basic economic unit, the household, which is discussed in Chapter 4. Household viability is not an easy term to define; I have used it to mean what the villagers themselves regard as a minimum—enough money to buy food to supplement that which is grown, to pay taxes, and buy one new set of clothes a year for each member of the household. However, mainly because of the poor copra yields and prices in 1966, few households achieved even this minimum. About 67 per cent of households in the village fell below it, 20 per cent just about maintained it, and a further 13 per cent had a surplus. In a good year, obviously more households would achieve viability or even a surplus.

Even making allowance for the abnormally low income from copra, these figures do reinforce the point that there are considerable inequalities in the distribution of wealth, although, as is often remarked, 'There are no rich men in Minazini.' In fact, only a very old and crippled person will not depend for food largely on his or her own efforts as a cultivator.

CHAPTER 2

DESCENT GROUPS
AND PERSONAL NETWORKS

In many areas of social activity Minazini villagers act as members of corporate, unrestricted, cognatic descent groups. The first part of this chapter describes the formal structure of these groups, showing how members are recruited and new groups formed, and mentions briefly the contexts in which they function as social units.

However, the villagers do not always see themselves acting only as members of descent groups or their constituent segments, but also as part of one another's *jamaa* or personal network, which is made up primarily of kin, but also includes affines, friends, and neighbours.

The structure of the descent groups

Six named cognatic descent groups (*vikao*, sing. *kikao*) function in the contexts of land-holding, residence, marriage, and spirit possession. The method of recruitment to all of the groups is by birth, and all the known descendants of the apical ancestor, through both men and women, are recognized as members of the group. Furthermore, membership is on the basis of ascription only; it is not necessary to reside with the group or affiliate with it in some other way in order to claim membership.[1] The Minazini descent groups are thus 'unrestricted' or 'open' in terms of residence or other methods of affiliation; they are also unrestricted by sex, since membership is traced through both men and women.

Descent groups in Minazini may be defined as corporate according to most of the definitions commonly used by lawyers and anthropologists: continuity and the exercise of common rights (Maine 1888); the regulation of the group by administrative authority (Weber 1957); the control of collective property, the existence of authoritative representation, and the occasional meeting of the group (Radcliffe-Brown 1950); the collective exercise of a set of rights and the acceptance of a set of duties (Firth 1959). The only possible argument against the corporateness of the groups is that they are not discrete; thus, they do not conform to one of Weber's criteria, that corporate groups must be exclusive.

A descent group can be shown in a single genealogy, since all of its members are descended from a single ancestor.[2] However, this does not mean that all the members know how to trace their relationship to one another, since some of the descent groups are very large. The largest group, F,[3] has a depth of ten generations, group C follows with eight generations, groups A, B, and D have seven each, while group E, which split off from group A, has only six generations. Kinship is usually recognized to the third and fourth generations above ego, and to this degree people are able to trace their relationship fairly exactly. Of people with whom there is a more distant connection they will merely say 'we are brothers' (ndugu). In each descent group, there is a small handful of older men whom I propose to term 'Elders'. They are referred to as wazee wakubwa (important old men) because they know the genealogy of the descent group, having been themselves taught by a former Elder. These men tend to act as informal leaders and representatives of the descent groups on certain occasions. (It should be noted that not all old men (wazee) are automatically Elders and thus considered to be repositories of genealogical information, although of course older people, women as well as men, know more about such matters than younger ones.) Thus as long as a person can find an Elder who will validate his or her claim to be descended from the founder of the descent group, he or she retains rights therein. Only if the genealogical link has been forgotten by all the Elders, will a claim be denied.

What are the functions of the descent groups? One of the most important is that they hold land, both residential and cultivable. Minazini people themselves emphasize the close relationship between land and descent groups in explaining the existence of the six groups in the village today. They say that originally the six descent groups formed separate hamlets scattered around the present village site. The members of each hamlet recognized themselves as descendants of a single ancestor or ancestress, who had established rights over the land of the hamlet. Other people might have come to live in the hamlet on sufferance, and possibly have married a hamlet member. In such a case, the children would have had full rights as members of the hamlet. The villagers say that when the descent groups lived separately they were almost entirely endogamous units and did not intermarry as they do today (see below).

To some extent, this explanation is substantiated by the little historical evidence available, chiefly the map drawn by Baumann in 1896, which shows five hamlet names grouped around the present village site. All of these names are in use today, but most of the former hamlets are no longer inhabited; the lands are merely used for the cultivation of annual crops. Three of Baumann's hamlet names coincide with the names of present-day descent groups in Minazini, and the land shown on the map to be associated with them is still claimed by these groups. However, only one descent group is still living on the site of the old hamlet. The area once occupied by another group, in the north of the village, was taken over by some German settlers, and the former inhabitants went to live in the south of the present village. The F group people, who are shown as living on a ridge to the east of the present village, now live within the village itself, and only return to their original home to cultivate land. Graves and wells on the ridge testify to their former occupancy. The members of this group say that they came down into the present village because the German colonial administration insisted that every man should plant at least 50 coconut trees, and the soil on the ridge was not suitable. This indeed may be the reason why the hamlets moved closer together, thus forming a single village, since the sandy soil in and around the present village site is so much more suitable for the growing of coconuts than that farther afield.

Today, the village is divided into named wards, each one of which is associated with a descent group (cf. map of the village). Most of the people living in a ward are members of the descent group which holds the land, or else are married into this group (cf. Chapter 3). Most bush lands surrounding the village are likewise divided among the descent groups, and rights to these lands are obtained through descent group membership. This is discussed in detail in Chapter 4.

Apart from functioning as land-holding units, descent groups act corporately on certain occasions. Thus, for example, when kinship rituals, such as marriages, funeral and puberty rites are held, the cooking is carried out by women grouped according to descent. Each woman is affiliated with a cooking group soon after her marriage, and continues to cook with this group for the rest of her life. Her cooking group is one of the descent groups of which she is a member. Usually, if the parents belong to different descent groups, and there are several daughters, each girl affiliates with a different cooking group, although she still remains a member of several descent groups.

In addition to such regular occasions as those mentioned above, the descent groups can function as social units on other occasions. For example, during the war rations were distributed according to descent group membership; furthermore, if any compulsory labour was required by the government, men worked in gangs composed of fellow descent group members.

The descent groups are internally differentiated into segments known variously as *matumbo*, *milango*, and *makoo* (sing. *tumbo*, *mlango*, and *koo*). The word *tumbo*, which literally means 'stomach' or 'womb', is defined in northern Mafia as the children of one mother or one father, and can be applied to a unit several generations in depth. It is in fact through membership of a *tumbo* that a person is a member of a descent group, and many rights and duties are defined by *tumbo* membership, rather than by membership of the *kikao* as a whole. Thus for example, the large named fields which are held by the descent groups are in fact allocated on the basis of *tumbo* membership; people do not have rights to all of the land of their *vikao*. The same also applies to spirit possession; men and women are possessed by the same spirits as possessed their ancestors. Thus a person can be possessed only by the spirit which is associated with his or her particular *tumbo*.

A *tumbo*, then, may be defined as the descendants of one man or woman; it can vary in depth from two to ten generations, and its exact composition is clear only in context. Much the same definition applies to the *makoo* and *milango*. In some parts of the coast,[4] *koo*, like *tumbo*, has the connotation of femaleness, but on Mafia it is used to refer to the descendants of both men and women. It is used in Minazini synonymously with *tumbo*, and occasionally it is also a synonym for *kikao*. *Mlango*, which literally means 'door', is also used in northern Mafia with the same meaning as *tumbo* and *koo*. As one old man in Minazini said to me '*koo* and *tumbo* and *mlango* are just different words; they have the same meaning'. In this book I do not propose to make any distinction between them, and will thus use only the word *tumbo* to refer to segments of a descent group.

Descent groups and their constituent segments differ in a number of important ways. The first is that descent groups are named entities, whereas segments are referred to only by the name of their apical ancestor. The second point is that descent groups are fixed units; their boundaries do not vary according to context, whereas a segment can be of almost any size, although, generally speaking, it refers to a unit three to four generations in depth.

Another important distinction between the descent groups and the segments is that members of the former cannot all trace their relationship to one another. Members of segments, on the other hand, unless the segment has an unusually great depth, generally know how they are related. Thus members of a person's segment are also usually part of his or her kinship universe (*jamaa*), whereas members of the same descent group who do not share segment membership could fall outside the *jamaa*.

Segments occasionally break off from a parent descent group and form an independent descent group; this has already happened in the case of group E which hived off from group A. It is difficult to obtain information about why this descent group split in this way, as the split appears to have taken place some time ago. However it may have coincided with the introduction of the *tarika* societies (Sufi mystical orders) (cf. Chapter 5), and the division of the village into two rival societies. Group A supported the leader of one society, and group E the other, and in fact the village leaders of the two societies belong respectively to the two descent groups.

Even now descent group A appears to be in the process of splitting yet again; one of its segments has moved away from the southern ward, to another location, just by the point where the fair weather motorable track to the village finishes, and another track leads on to a neighbouring village. I shall refer to this segment as the Crossroads segment. On occasion I have heard people refer to this segment as if it were an independent descent group, and claim that there are seven, not six descent groups in the village. The attempt of this segment to split off from the main group is symbolized not only by moving to a separate ward, but also by the building of a separate daily mosque, although it still acts as a constituent part of group A in other contexts, such as land-holding. Group E, on the other hand, which has definitely established its independence of group A, does not interact in any of these contexts with its parent group.

Group B also appears to be in the process of splitting. One segment remains in the northern part of the village, where Baumann (ibid.) placed it over 70 years ago, but another segment has moved to the southern part of the village, and its members interact largely with the neighbouring people of descent group A. However members of both northern and southern segments still call themselves members of the B descent group, and hold cultivable land in common (cf. Chapter 4).

Since descent groups are no longer, if indeed they ever were (as the Minazini people claim), completely endogamous, it is obvious that a man or woman, whose parents were members of different descent groups, can claim membership of as many groups as could his or her parents. As this is a cumulative process, it might be expected that over a period of time most people would be able to claim membership in all the descent groups in the village (and, given inter-village marriage, membership of groups in other villages too). In fact, this is not the case, as Table 5 shows.

TABLE 5
Descent group membership

Name of descent group	No. of members (male and female)	% of adult population
A	77	16
B	125	26
C	58	12
D	106	22
E	84	17
F	222	46

Notes: 1. These numbers include adult men and women who are living in Minazini; there are many other members of Minazini descent groups who live in other villages.

2. Membership is defined by a person's appearing on the genealogy given by one or more descent group Elders.

The principal factor which prevents everyone becoming a member of every group is preferential kin marriage, usually between cousins. Since any two people who are kin also share membership of at least one descent group, it follows that their children are members of fewer descent groups than if their parents had been unrelated. Conversely, given that people are members of fewer descent groups than they might have been, had not their parents shared a common descent group membership, it also follows that the groups themselves are smaller than if such a type of marriage were not practised.

However before going on to consider marriage and the way in which it affects the membership and structure of the descent groups, I want first to consider the *jamaa*, for in fact people usually view marriage as taking place between kin or non-kin, rather than between people who are or are not members of the same descent group.

The jamaa

The links with which a person is surrounded are referred to as the *jamaa*. This is a difficult word to translate, since its meaning can vary considerably according to context, but basically, it means an ego-centred grouping. At its widest, it may mean all the people with whom ego has ties of kinship, affinity, neighbourhood, and friendship; this I have called the 'personal network'. Secondly, it may also refer more narrowly to ego's kinship universe (*jamaa wanaohusiana*—the people who are related), that is all the people with whom he or she traces a genealogical relationship. In most cases, an ego's kinship universe is completely bi-lateral. This is true in most societies, but it is to be expected that in a society with cognatic descent groups, fairly equal importance should be attached to maternal and paternal kin. This is emphasized in the kinship terminology which makes no distinction between paternal and maternal kin, and in which men and women use the same terms of reference. The important distinctions are between generations, and, to a lesser extent, between juniors and seniors within a generation.

The kinship universe normally includes the members of an individual's descent group segments, unless these are exceptionally large, but does not include all fellow-members of a descent group or groups, since kinship links cannot always be traced with them. The *jamaa* in this second sense thus cuts across the boundaries of the different descent groups to which most people belong, i.e. members of different descent groups are brought together by being included in the same *jamaa*. This is particularly true on the occasion of a wedding or funeral or other ritual, when in fact *jamaa* may be translated by yet a third term, that of 'action set' (cf. Mayer 1966) brought together for that particular purpose.

The boundaries of an ego's *jamaa* (of whatever type) vary with time. An older person is likely to have a much larger *jamaa* than a younger one. This is largely because the size of ego's kinship universe increases over time, both because of the birth of children and grandchildren, and also because people tend to learn more of their genealogies as they grow older through participation in rituals and being taught by Elders, so that their recognized collateral ties also become wider.

One old man in his seventies gave me his personal genealogy; this stretched back to four generations above himself, and three below. Undoubtedly, he could call up a large action set, and indeed, at the marriage of his grand-daughter, he did so (see below). Another informant, a middle-aged woman, knew about her grandparents and some of their siblings, but knew little about her great-grandparents.

Younger informants knew much less—a young man around thirty knew only his grandparents and their descendants, but nothing about his grandparents' siblings, much less his great-grandparents. And the same was true of this man's wife. So that if this couple wished to activate an action set, say for the circumcision of one of their sons, they would call upon their parents to activate *their* personal networks and undertake most of the arrangements.

Age is not the only factor in the size of an ego's personal network; status is also important, although in this society few people gain status in any field before they reach middle-age. For the boundaries of the personal network do not depend only upon whom ego recognizes, but also upon the people who agree to be included. Thus an old and respected man of high status, like the first informant mentioned above, who is not only a descent group Elder but also Imam (leader of prayers) of the Friday mosque, would have a larger personal network, and thus be able to call up a larger action set than a man of the same age who is of little account in the village. Similarly, the middle-aged woman, mentioned above, who is prominent in a spirit possession guild, would have a larger personal network than a woman of the same age who is of no importance.

The size of the *jamaa* as action set depends not only upon the foregoing factors, but also upon context; a small kinship ritual, such as a Koranic reading for a dead parent (cf. Chapter 5) brings together a much smaller action set to help with the arrangements than a larger ritual such as a wedding or funeral. The former type of ritual would include only those people called 'close *jamaa*' (*jamaa sana*), whereas for the latter type of ritual a man or woman would try to include as many members of their personal network as possible, as is shown below.

The point is then that descent groups and the *jamaa* provide two separate frameworks, although a distinction is not always made between them. Villagers often see themselves acting as members of one another's *jamaa* rather than as descent group members; however, the workings of the *jamaa* affect the structure of the descent groups, as a consideration of marriage practices demonstrates.

Marriage and divorce

Marriage in Minazini is conducted according to Islamic law and, in particular, according to the tenets of the Shafei school. It is considered a normal and desirable state to be married, and almost every girl weds soon after puberty, while few boys remain unmarried beyond their very early twenties. The only adults in Minazini who have never been married are two men who have spent long periods in Zanzibar, and returned to the village without wives, and two young girls who are blind. But even in cases of quite severe handicaps a spouse is normally found.

Under Islamic law, men may marry up to four wives at any one time, but only a minority of men in the village are polygynously married; 22, or 10 per cent of the adult male population have two wives, and one man has three wives. However, divorce (which is discussed later in this chapter), is extremely frequent, and in fact serial polygamy is the norm for both men and women.

The most prestigious form of marriage is with a young girl, who is expected to be a virgin. Normally such girls marry youths also marrying for the first time. The first marriages of young people are arranged by parents and grandparents, and are attended by great celebrations, with both parties incurring great expense. Subsequent marriages, when the couple generally please themselves as to choice of partner, are much smaller affairs.

It is normally first marriages which take place between close kin. The commonest form of preferential kin marriage is between cross-cousins (*binamu*); they have a joking relationship and if a girl does not marry one of her cross-cousins, then at her wedding he has the right to claim a small sum of money (*ugongo*—usually 10 cents) from the groom. Similarly, a girl can demand that her male cross-cousin, if not marrying her, should pay her *ugongo* when he marries. Patrilateral parallel cousin marriage is almost as frequent as is cross-cousin marriage (see Table 6), but matrilateral parallel cousin marriage is extremely rare, except among the Arabs, and a few who identify themselves with them. Kin marriage is not however restricted to members of the same generation, and there are instances of men marrying their classificatory mothers, daughters, and grand-daughters.

Out of the total of 380 marriages contracted by male villagers, 80 (21 per cent) took place between close kin (defined as having a common ancestor not more than three generations back). A further 10 per cent took place between kin who are more distantly related, but who would nonetheless be able to trace the relationship, and would probably call each other by a kinship term prior to marriage. However, if the figures had been restricted to the 208 *first* marriages of village males, we would find that the incidence of kin marriage is even higher, with 36 per cent taking place between close kin (as already defined), and a further 9 per cent between more distant kin. Thus, in the case of first marriages, 45 per cent take place between kin who are close enough to trace a relationship, and who also, of course, share a common descent group membership.

TABLE 6
Incidence of kin marriage

(*a*) with a patrilateral parallel cousin	21
(*b*) with a patrilateral cross-cousin	23
(*c*) with a matrilateral cross-cousin	20
(*d*) with a matrilateral parallel cousin	6
(*e*) with a classificatory daughter	8
(*f*) with a classificatory mother	1
(*g*) with a distant relative	41
(*h*) with an unrelated person	260
Total marriages	380 (100%)

Note: These figures [5] are for all marriages of men resident in the village.

What are the reasons for this type of preferential marriage? Minazini people say that marriage with kin is a good thing for several reasons—firstly, the families concerned are bound to know each other well; secondly, any marital disputes can be settled without recourse to non-family members; thirdly, that such marriages are more stable than those between non-kin; and finally, that they help prevent fragmentation of coconut groves (cf. Chapter 3).

The first reason is obviously valid, although it may happen that kin marriages take place over fairly wide distances as in the instance of the Imam's grand-daughter's marriage discussed below. However, by 'knowing each other well', villagers mean primarily that they know about each other's ancestry and status, and can thus avoid, for example, unwittingly marrying off a child to someone who has some slave ancestry.

The second point would also seem to be borne out by my observations. At least six cases of disputes between husband and wife who were unrelated came before the Village Development Council during my stay, but only one case between a husband and wife who were kin, and even this was in exceptional circumstances. Marital quarrels between spouses who are kin are usually settled by an informal meeting of their relatives.

Obviously kin are not always successful in settling disputes, and quite a high proportion of kin marriages do end in divorce. However, it is true that fewer kin marriages than non-kin marriages end in divorce, as Table 7 shows.

TABLE 7

Comparison of rates of divorce in first marriages as between kin and non-kin

Marriages	Divorced	Deceased	Surviving	Total
Kin	23 (23%)	7 (7%)	70 (70%)	100 (100%)
Non-kin	40 (37%)	13 (12%)	55 (51%)	108 (100%)

Thus only 23 per cent of first marriages between kin end in divorce, compared with 37 per cent of first marriages between previously unrelated persons.[6]

Three effects of kin marriage may be distinguished. First of all, it helps to prevent the fragmentation of property on inheritance; secondly, it restricts the size of descent groups, by restricting the number of groups in which the offspring of such unions can claim membership; thirdly, if practised intensively, it creates a small circle of intra-marrying kin, who may employ this strategy to preserve their status (cf. Chapters 5 and 7).

Property, such as coconut trees, is inherited under Islamic law, and inheritance is the most frequent way of acquiring such property (cf. Table 11). Normally, however, a woman receives only half a man's portion. Sometimes women do receive an equal amount, either by agreement with their brothers, or because a dying parent has requested this (cf. Chapter 3). Obviously the effect of kin marriage is to keep property, particularly coconut trees, in the hands of a smaller range of kin than might otherwise happen. This does not mean that an individual necessarily receives a larger share, but that the holding is less fragmented, i.e. it tends to be concentrated in a single area rather than being scattered all over the village, or even over several villages. An important aspect of this is that the intra-marrying group has its trees in the same area, and thus is likely to reside together.

The second effect of kin marriage, as already mentioned, is that it restricts the size of the descent group in which it is practised, because the offspring of such marriages have claims to membership of fewer groups than they might have done if their parents had been un-related.

Figure 3 illustrates this point:

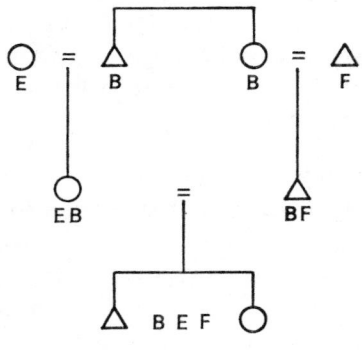

FIG. 3(a)

Kin marriage and descent group membership

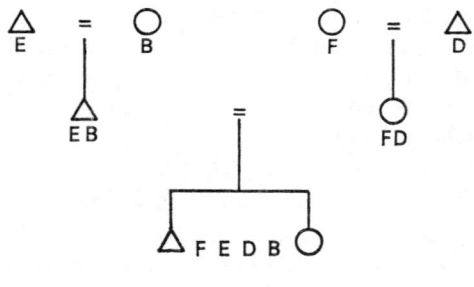

FIG. 3(b)

Non-kin marriage and descent group membership

Although the majority of such marriages are viewed by the villagers as taking place between kin (i.e. within the *jamaa*) rather than within the descent group, the fact remains that they have an effect on the descent groups themselves, as I have tried to show. However, apart from the 45 per cent of first marriages which take place between kin, a further 15 per cent take place between people who cannot necessarily trace a relationship, but who nonetheless share membership of at least one descent group. This means that approximately 60 per cent of first marriages are endogamous, and this factor obviously reduces considerably the number of people who can claim membership in different groups.

However, this high rate of endogamy in the case of first marriages is somewhat mitigated in its effects by a high divorce and re-marriage rate. Men in the village aged sixty years or more (i.e. who are unlikely to marry again) have had an average of 2·75 wives per head during their lifetimes, and women of the same age have had only slightly fewer husbands, an average of just over 2 each. Divorce, particularly for men, is extremely easy to obtain, as only the Islamic formula of repudiation needs to be used. Women can either persuade their husbands to divorce them by making life unpleasant for them, or 'buy' their divorce, or else they can sue for divorce in the court in Kilindoni, usually on the grounds that their husbands do not maintain them adequately.

This high divorce and re-marriage rate means that a woman's closest ties are with her mother and/or brothers, and it is to them that she returns after divorce. Her own mother may not by this time be living with her father. Since children normally remain with their mothers when a couple separates, they often grow up among their maternal rather than paternal kin, and this has an effect on residence patterns, as the following chapter shows. Most important of all for the purposes of this discussion is that divorce mitigates the effects of kin marriages. Since many marriages between kin do end in divorce, and subsequent marriages are much less likely to take place between kin, many women bear children by men to whom they are not related, and with whom they do not share descent group membership, and the children of such marriages are therefore likely to be members of several descent groups.

In sum then, because the descent groups in Minazini are unrestricted, many people can claim membership of more than one group. But the likelihood that anyone will be able to claim membership of all groups is small, because kin marriage, viewed as intra-descent group marriage, reduces the number of Minazini descent groups in which an individual can claim membership. This is seen in Table 8.

TABLE 8
Numbers of descent groups in which membership is claimed

	1 d/g	2 d/g	3 d/g	4 d/g	5 d/g	6 d/g	Total
Men	84	71	28	3	1	0	187
	(45%)	(38%)	(15%)	(1·5%)	(0·5%)		(100%)
Women	89	73	24	6	1	0	193
	(46%)	(38%)	(12·5%)	(3·0%)	(0·5%)		(100%)

This table deals only with those persons in Minazini who are members of the six descent groups in the village. Arabs, descendants of slaves, Gunya, and immigrants from other areas are not included. Some 23 men (11 per cent of the total male population) and 81 women (30 per cent of the total female population) are not included because they do not have claims to membership of any of the Minazini descent groups (the reason for the much higher proportion of women with no descent group membership is that many of them are married in from other villages).

Of those who are members of Minazini descent groups, roughly the same proportions of men as women are members of between two and five groups, and just over half of the men, and nearly 40 per cent of the women in the village have some choice about affiliation because they are members of more than one group.

There are two possibilities open to people with membership of more than one group. One is to affiliate solely with one of their groups, and drop all effective ties with the rest. This may be carried to the extent of marrying off one's children within that group, thus effectively giving grandchildren a more limited choice of membership, and attempting to ensure that they act mainly within the chosen group. As will be seen, this is done by a large minority mainly for status reasons (cf. Chapters 5 and 7). The second possibility is to exercise rights in some or all of the descent groups of which one is a member: to affiliate with different groups at different times and in different contexts. As will be seen, this is the course of action which a majority of people choose. However, in spite of the importance of descent group membership in so many contexts, people do not always see themselves acting primarily as members of descent groups. Many of their actions are explained rather in terms of the *jamaa*, even though, as in the case of marriage choices, the structure of the descent groups is ultimately affected. In order further to demonstrate the way in which these two frameworks—the descent groups and the *jamaa*—interrelate, I propose to examine marriage from another angle—that of the payments which surround it.

Descent group and jamaa: *The economics of marriage*

The marriage of a young girl involves considerable expense, which is borne by both the bride's and groom's families. However, if the groom is marrying for the second or subsequent time, he usually has to find most of the payments himself. This is probably one of the main reasons why men seeking second or subsequent wives tend not to marry young girls, as it is very difficult for them to find all the necessary payments without the help of kin.

The groom's payments consist firstly of those required by Islamic law, that is the marriage payment (*mahari*) paid to the bride herself, or at least promised her at the time of the wedding. Usually this is around 150s.–200s., although occasionally it may be as low as 100s., particularly in the case of a divorced or widowed woman. The groom also has to provide the bride with a complete trousseau (*sanduku*—box) which can hardly cost less than several hundred shillings for a bride's first marriage.

In addition to the money spent on the bride there are other people to whom the groom has to make payments. First is the bride's father, to whom a payment of around 100s., known as 'turban' (*kilemba*)[7] is made. Prior to this, at the time of the betrothal, the groom has to pay the father 'letter money' (*pesa za barua*), i.e. he encloses 10s. or 20s. in the formal letter proposing marriage. Between the betrothal and marriage, he makes frequent visits to his fiancée's parents, and takes gifts of food, etc.

Secondly, he has to give the bride's mother between 50s. and 100s., a sum which is known as 'belt' (*mkaja*).[8] Thirdly, he has to pay the go-between (*mposaji*) who conducts the initial negotiations around 50s. if the match is brought to a successful conclusion.

Finally, before he is allowed to enter the bridal chamber and consummate the marriage, he has to pay the girl's *mkunga* (sexual instructress, who is usually the father's sister) a fee (*kipa mkono*) which must be a minimum of 30s. and may be much higher.

The total costs for a groom are shown in Table 9.

When it is remembered that the average annual cash income for men is rarely more than 200s.–300s. per annum (cf. Chapter 1), it can

TABLE 9
Groom's marriage expenses

Mahari	200s.
Sanduku (trousseau)	250s.
Letter money	10s.
Food, gifts between betrothal and marriage	50s.
Kilemba to father	100s.
Mkaja to mother	75s.
Kipa mkono to *mkunga*	50s.
Payment to go-between	50s.
Total costs	785s.

be seen that marriage needs a considerable outlay, and it would not be possible to raise such amounts without the help of kin.

The bride's family also have heavy expenses to bear. Normally her parents provide a complete set of household furniture and utensils, including the marital double bed, an ornate and expensive item. In addition they have to bear the cost of the marriage feast. The *mkunga* may provide a separate set of household utensils, or she may contribute to those bought by the bride's parents. She also has to cook at least one pot of rice and meat at the marriage feast for the groom and his party. However, both the parents and *mkunga* know that they will receive money from the groom and they do not have to find all the costs themselves. Even so, this is unlikely to be sufficient, and they too will have to call on the help of relatives.

The kinship universe surrounding a bride or groom is seen by people in Minazini as consisting of four categories. The first category is known as the *wenyewe* (lit. 'themselves', sing. *mwenyewe*); these are some of the very close kin. They are invited to discuss proposals, and they thus constitute an action set from the start. The *wenyewe* have a say in all decisions made, and in planning the wedding itself. Normally the *wenyewe* would include the parents of the bride or groom, parents' siblings, parents' parents, and their siblings.

The second category consists of the close kin and affines of the *wenyewe* themselves. These are invited to the 'drying of the rice' a few days before the wedding. This invitation means that a contribution of money and/or food is expected. This category is referred to as *jamaa sana*—close *jamaa*—and these people generally remain in or around the house where the wedding is being held for two or three days before the ceremony takes place.

On the day after the 'drying of the rice' is held, another task, the 'pounding of the rice', is performed. Again, people are invited by the *wenyewe*, rather than by the father or mother of the bride, but these are still people who are included in the kinship universe of the latter. They are referred to as *jamaa wanaohusiana*—'the *jamaa* who are related'; they do not necessarily make any kind of contribution, and if they do, it is usually a small one.

Each of the *mwenyewe* invites to the wedding members of his or her personal network. These people attend only the wedding ceremony itself and the feast, and they do not make any sort of contribution.

Contributions, whether of money or food, are rarely made direct to the givers of the rituals. The *wenyewe* collect from their relatives by saying 'I have a wedding (or funeral, or puberty ceremony, as the case may be), so please help me.' Note that the stress is on 'my' wedding, and the person is being asked to help the *mwenyewe*, and not necessarily the one holding the ritual. Each of the people approached by the *mwenyewe* will also approach members of his or her *jamaa* for help. The rule is that the more distant the relationship between the *mwenyewe* and those approached, the less is given. People who are not closely related put their contributions together and it is usually the head of the descent group segment in turn who hands them over to the *mwenyewe*.

In order to explain this more clearly I shall refer to a wedding organized by the Imam (leader of prayers) of the Friday mosque, who is one of the most important people in the village. In 1966 he arranged the marriage of his son's daughter to the grandson of his half-brother. The groom and his family had long been settled in Kwale, an island lying between Mafia and the mainland. Thus contact between the two families was minimal, because of geographical distance, but had been maintained, and was being renewed through this marriage.

The number of people who attended this wedding was extraordinarily large, the feasting and dancing lasted several days, instead of the usual twenty-four hours. A great deal of money was spent on both sides. The Imam first of all issued invitations to the *wenyewe*, and each of them had asked members of his or her personal network (usually close kin, but also possibly including more distant kin, affines or neighbours) to contribute.

It should perhaps be pointed out at this stage that the size of the contributions is determined not only by genealogical proximity, but also by geography. Kin who live at a distance drop their ties sooner than those living in the same village. When the Imam arranged the marriage of one of his own daughters, some twenty years earlier, he was able to invite relatives from Koma, another island lying between Mafia and the mainland. People remarked on the fact that they not only came, but actually made a contribution; this demonstrated clearly the large action-set which the Imam could call up. However, these people did not come to the marriage of the Imam's grand-daughter in 1966, and he admitted regretfully that the link had become rather weak by this time. However, he thought that had these people been living in Mafia, this would not have happened.

Another factor which affects the way in which individuals make use of their kinship universe is personal likes and dislikes. The father's brother's son of the Imam was not able to call on his sister's children to make contributions to him as a *mwenyewe* because of a quarrel between the Imam and their father's brother. In this particular instance, it is possible that the quarrel will either be made up or else will die with these two old men. Should the quarrel persist, and the link be broken, the two sides say of each other, 'We don't help with contributions to each other's rituals any more.'

Sometimes a link which is in danger of being forgotten may be deliberately resuscitated, as in the case of the marriage of the Imam's grand-daughter to a man from a place as distant as Kwale.

In such a context as a marriage, an ego's *jamaa* is a unity, in relation to the focal *ego*, and yet it is also split, because each member belongs to the *jamaa* of other people who may make competing demands for help. Thus when the grand-daughter of the Imam married, the groom's party called on the Imam, as the classificatory father of the groom's father, to contribute to the payment of the fee of the sexual instructress. The Imam borrowed the money, and handed it over to his 'son' (the groom's father). However a further 10s. was still required to make up the amount. The Imam obtained it from his own son, who was also the bride's father, and from two of his daughters, one of whom was the sexual instructress herself. The latter was thereby contributing to her own payment!

The Imam had also on the same occasion to contribute to a number of people who formed the *jamaa* of the bride's father, mother, and others. For example, he had to help his own daughter, who, as sexual instructress, bought household utensils for the bride. He also had to contribute to his classificatory grand-daughter, the mother of the groom, who bought a second trousseau for the bride.

Weddings, then, provide a good example of the way in which the *jamaa*, in all its meanings, operates. However, when talking about this wedding, the Imam switched frequently from talking about the *jamaa*, to talking in terms of descent groups and segments. For instance, some of the *wenyewe* he saw primarily as heads of segments, and he referred to the contributions of these people as coming from the segment, rather than from the members of the *mwenyewe's jamaa*. Similarly, some of the people who are not closely related to the Imam but who came to the wedding nonetheless, and even made a small contribution, he saw acting as members of descent groups.

Some of these people were members of descent groups D and E, and of another descent group in a neighbouring village. The Imam himself is a member of groups B and D, as well as of group A, and of the aforementioned group in another village. He pointed out that his closest ties are with groups A and B, since he obtains membership of

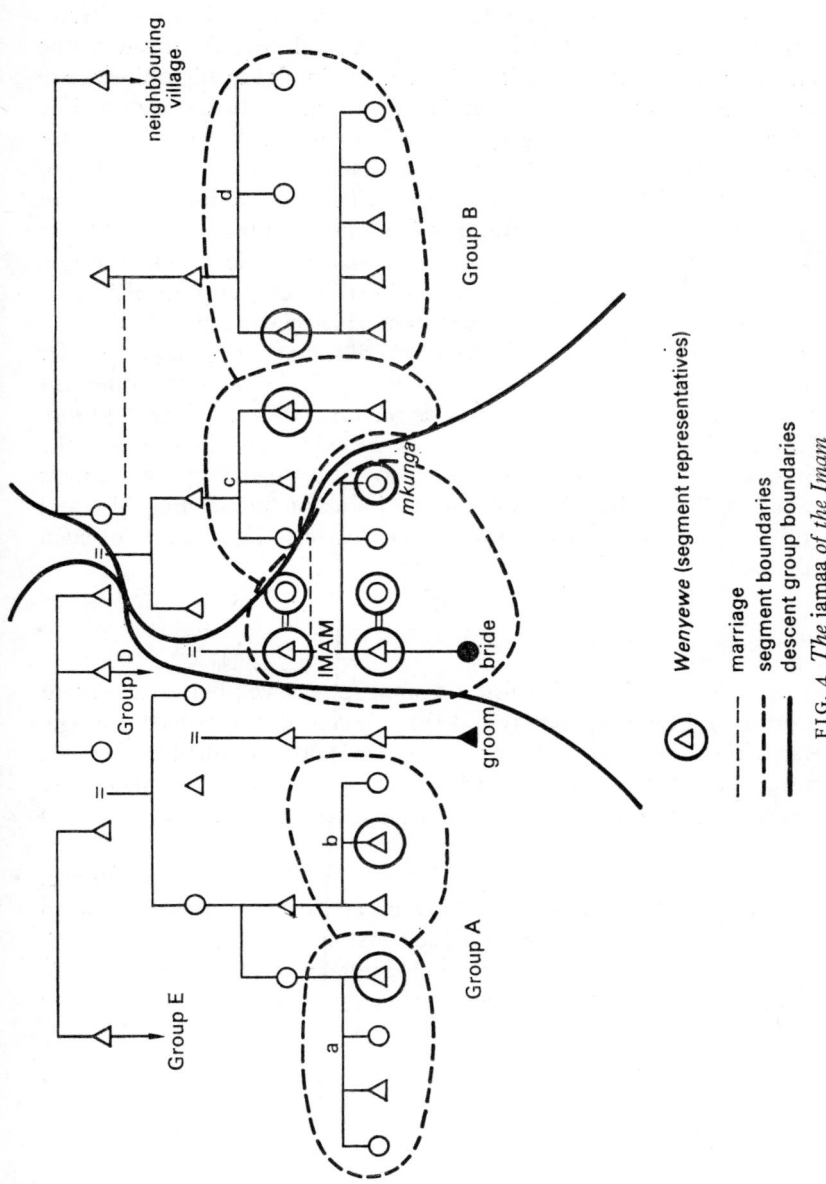

neighbouring village

Group B

d

c

mkunga

Group D

Group E

IMAM

bride

groom

b

a

Group A

Wenyewe (segment representatives)

——— marriage

--------- segment boundaries

- - - - descent group boundaries

———— descent group boundaries

FIG. 4 *The jamaa of the Imam*

these groups through several ancestors, whereas he is a member of group D and the group from the other village only through one ancestor. Thus most of the people included in his kinship universe are members of descent groups A and B. Furthermore, he interacts mainly with these two descent groups—he lives in an A group ward for instance. As a result, he saw the contributions made by members of group D and the group from another village as coming *from descent groups* 'as a whole'. Of course, this does not mean that he thought that *all* the members of group D, for instance, made a contribution, merely that he saw the people who did so as 'D group people'.

The reason why a contribution was made by some people who are members of descent group E is slightly different. As explained earlier in this chapter, descent group E originally broke away from descent group A. In all respects it acts as an independent descent group. However, in certain contexts, it may be advantageous to stress the original relationship between the two groups—the Imam perhaps asked for a contribution by using the idiom of this relationship, and the givers of the contribution complied because he is a man of such high status.

Conclusion

People can and do distinguish, on an abstract level, between descent groups (and their segments) and their *jamaa*. But in everyday usage, the distinction between these frameworks is often implied by context, rather than being made explicit, or else is not made at all, largely because the personnel in each of these categories overlaps to such a considerable extent.

But because the *jamaa* also includes such non-kin as affines, neighbours, and friends, it provides an alternative source of help to the descent groups, not only in such matters as collecting money to finance a marriage, but even in such contexts as residence and land-holding, the subjects of the next two chapters.

CHAPTER 3

RESIDENCE PATTERNS

Ward land and non-ward land

Land in Minazini may be categorized into three main types: (1) Residential ward land around the centre of the village, consisting of coconut plantations on sandy soil and meadow land, which is flooded in the wet season. This kind of land is held by descent groups. (2) Non-ward land, which is not associated with descent groups; there are two sub-categories of this: land to the north and east of the village, which is used both for cultivation and residence, and, secondly, land on the western side of the village, where coconut trees were first planted during German times, but which is not considered suitable for residence because of its distance from the village, and lack of a good water supply. (3) Bush land, used solely for the cultivation of annual crops; this lies on a fertile ridge to the east of the village. Most of this land is held by descent groups, and is discussed in the next chapter.

So far I have used the Swahili term *kikao* to mean a descent group. Etymologically, it is connected with the verb *kukaa*, meaning 'to live in a place', and the noun *kikao* is also used to refer to residential land held by a particular descent group. I have translated *kikao* in this sense by the term 'ward'.

Some descent groups hold more than one ward; in such cases it is a large segment of the descent group which is associated with the ward. Groups A, B, and D each hold two wards.

The right to live in a ward is conferred by two factors—one is membership of the descent group or segment associated with that ward, and the second is ownership of coconut trees within that ward. Ideally, these two factors should coincide. To what extent do they? Table 10 shows how many men own coconut trees on (*a*) ward land held by a descent group of which they are members; (*b*) ward land held by a descent group of which they are *not* members; and (*c*) non-ward land, i.e. land not held by any descent group.

From the table, it can be seen that approximately one third of the adult men own coconut trees only on ward land held by descent groups of which they are members (i.e. (*a*) type). An additional 15 per cent own trees both on their own ward land, and also on non-ward land which has been more recently planted up (i.e. (*a*) plus (*c*) type). A further 7 per cent own trees on non-ward land only (i.e. (*c*) type). In other words, there is no conflict here between ownership of coconut trees and descent group membership.

TABLE 10

Ownership of coconut trees and descent group membership

Kind of holding	No. of men owning trees	%
(*a*)	66	31·4
(*a*) plus (*c*)	32	15·2
(*b*)	17	8·1
(*c*)	15	7·1
(*b*) plus (*c*)	11	5·2
(*a*) plus (*b*)	10	4·9
(*a*) plus (*b*) plus (*c*)	6	2·9
own no trees	53	25·2
total adult male population	210	100

total men owning trees on			(*a*) land	114 (54%)
,,	,,	,,	(*b*) ,,	44 (21%)
,,	,,	,,	(*c*) ,,	64 (30·5%)

However, a further 44 men, or 21 per cent do own trees on ward land where they do not have descent group membership. This conflict of norms raises several questions, among which are firstly, how did these men acquire trees on such land, and secondly, do they utilize the rights conferred by ownership of trees to reside on ward land where they do not also have descent group membership?

In fact, 15 of these 44 men are not members of any descent group in Minazini. Some of them are immigrants from other villages, and some are descendants of slaves. But this still leaves a number of men who own trees in places where they might not be expected to do so. Before going on to see to what extent such men actually reside on ward land to which descent group membership does not entitle them, we might first consider how trees are acquired.

Means of acquiring coconut trees

The chief means of acquiring coconut trees are inheritance, purchase, and planting. As previously stated, under Islamic law trees are inherited by both men and women, although a woman receives only half of a man's portion. Furthermore, husbands and wives can also inherit from each other, but while a husband gets a quarter of his deceased wife's property, a wife receives only one-eighth of her husband's. However, women do have one extra source of trees, and that is through the marriage payment (*mahari*) made to them either at the time of marriage or else when the marriage is dissolved by divorce or death. Since, on the whole, women live longer than men, they are more likely to inherit trees from their husbands than *vice versa*.

Trees are mostly planted by younger couples, who often move out of the village on to non-ward land, where anyone can settle. There is little opportunity to plant new trees on ward land, which is almost completely planted up. However, living on non-ward land has its drawbacks; it is isolated from the social life of the village, and people tend to dislike living there for this reason. Furthermore, it involves men in full-time agricultural work—cultivating annual crops, cassava, and planting coconut trees all in the same area, and usually this leaves little time for other activities, such as fishing, or casual labouring work, which brings in a small cash income. It takes at least seven years before a coconut tree begins to bear, and during the early years the young trees have to be carefully watched, lest they be damaged by wild pigs. In short, then, planting coconut trees is a long-term project, and few young men can afford to wait seven years for cash returns for their efforts. The fact remains, however, that of the people residing on non-ward land the majority are young men, who will probably remain living there until their fathers and/or mothers die, leaving them some trees in the village. During the period of study, the majority of persons moving house were young men shifting from the village to non-ward land, or *vice versa*.

Buying trees is also a possibility for some men. Generally, it is older men who are in a position to do this—either men who already own trees, and have a source of income, not all of which is consumed by household expenses, or else who are successful traders. Women and young men are very rarely in a position to buy trees, as a single tree costs at least 20s. It is a little difficult to generalize about the frequency with which trees change hands, because, as already remarked, the years during which this study was made were very dry, and the trees were bearing very little, so that few people had spare cash with which to buy trees, and in any case, since there was so little profit to be made from them, it was hardly worthwhile. However, some trees were bought and sold, and there appeared to be two motives for selling. One was sheer lack of cash; several people sold a few trees here and there to make ends meet. Generally this is condemned by everyone, as it is realized that a person who does this rarely has the means of buying them back. Several elderly men in the village were represented as dire warnings to the younger; they were said to have owned plenty of trees at one time, but then gradually to have sold them off.

Thus it is that most people who have trees on ward lands where they do not also have descent group membership (i.e. (b) type holding) have purchased them. The oft-stated ideal in Minazini is that if a man must sell some of his coconut trees, a thing which is in itself highly undesirable, he must give pre-emptive rights to his neighbours, who are normally his close kin (*jamaa sana*) and then to other kinsmen. To sell land to non-kin is frowned on, as the following case shows:

CASE I

Selling land to strangers

S.A. was an only child when his father died, leaving him 66 coconut trees. The property was administered by the government office in Kilindoni, and leased to the boy's father's brother, who paid the rent into a trust fund in the government office. On coming of age, the boy was to take possession of his trees, and of the rent which had accrued during the years of his minority.

In 1966, four years after his father's death, S.A. was fifteen years old, and under Islamic law this meant that he had attained his majority, although it seems unlikely that this would have been recognized by the government officials administering his estate. S.A. was a shiftless youth, with no occupation, and he decided to sell all his trees in order to buy a bicycle. He did this without consulting any of his relatives. The buyer was not a kinsman, and he bought the trees for only 650s., when they were worth at least 2,000s. at the current market price.

S.A.'s father's brother's son, acting on behalf of the father's brother who had rented the trees, went to Kilindoni to petition that the sale was illegal on two counts. The first was that the boy was simple, and although theoretically an adult (at least under Islamic law) incapable of handling his own affairs. The second point was that the sale was void because neighbours had not been offered pre-emptive rights.

The case had not been decided before I left the field, as the boy had meanwhile been arrested and sentenced to a two-year term in prison for stealing.

This case illustrates the concern with which people view the sale of trees to non-kin. Almost all other sales that I heard about during my stay in the village were between kinsmen and/or neighbours. One exception is the following case, in which a man did sell coconut trees to an affine who was not a kinsman.

CASE 2

Selling trees to an affine

A.J. sold a few coconut trees in a large field which he owned to an affine, his daughter's husband, who lived in a neighbouring village. Shortly afterwards, the son-in-law wished to sell these trees in order to raise some cash, as he was in the process of purchasing a large field elsewhere. He offered to sell back the trees to A.J., who unfortunately had no money at the time. However, A.J. went round to all his relatives, saying what a terrible thing it would be if the trees were sold to strangers . . . In the end he managed to raise the necessary cash and buy the trees back.

A.J. managed to 'save' his trees by borrowing money from his relatives. Similarly, in the previous case, S.A.'s relatives emphasized that if it had been proved that the boy had a right to sell the trees, which they themselves doubted, then they would have taken steps to buy them themselves.

However there are exceptions to the above ideal. Firstly, affines may be able to get hold of coconut trees, as Case 2 shows. Secondly, a man sometimes sells to a kinsman who is not a member of the descent group associated with the ward in which the trees are located. Finally, it may be that a man desperate for money, and with no close kin to put pressure on him, or to help him financially, may sell to someone who is not a kinsman, but has ready cash. Thus it is quite possible for people to get trees on land not associated with one of their own descent groups. The second motive for selling is a more positive one, and this is to try to get one's trees all in the same place. If a man inherits trees in more than one area, and perhaps acquires trees by other methods such as planting, then he may well sell some of the trees, and buy others in the area in which he is actually living.

Inheritance, buying, and planting apart, a few people do acquire trees by other means, namely by gift, or renting.[1] The most common recipient of a gift is a daughter, particularly if she has no brothers.

This is because under Islamic law daughters may not inherit all their parents' property, and if a parent dies without sons some of the property has to pass to the nearest male heir, usually a brother's sons. Some parents therefore, before they die, give gifts to their daughters to mitigate this. Another method of ensuring that daughters get a larger share of property than is usual is by declaring property *wakf*, which means that it becomes an endowment which cannot be sold or divided. A *wakf*[2] may be made in favour of one or several persons, and if the latter then the profits must be shared equally. Of course, this device also prevents feckless sons from selling off their inheritance, and leaving themselves without any capital. Another method of helping daughters to receive an equal proportion of property is for a parent, usually on his death-bed, to ask his sons and daughters to keep the property as *shirika*. This institution is not recognized by Islamic law, but it means that the property remains undivided, and the profits are shared equally by sons and daughters. However, unlike *wakf*, which in theory at any rate is a perpetual endowment, *shirika* only lasts for a generation, and on the death of one of the holders has to be divided.

The only other method of obtaining trees is by renting. This is rarely done in Minazini, although it happens more frequently in the southern villages. In Minazini, a few women lease their trees to men; they may find it convenient to do this if they are married away from the village, and have no male relatives to look after their interests. Women on the whole are more loath to sell trees than men, because divorce is frequent and ownership provides them with some security when they are no longer supported by a husband. And since a husband is bound to support his wife, women are less likely than men to need to sell trees in order to cover recurrent expenses.

Table 11 shows how trees have been obtained in Minazini.

Let us return now to the relationship between descent groups and ownership of coconut trees on ward land. As Table 10 shows, 44 men own trees on ward land held by descent groups of which they are not members. To what extent do they reside on this land? Only half in fact do so, and eight of these are among those who are not members of any Minazini descent groups. In sum then, out of a total male population of 210 men, in only fourteen cases is there any conflict between the two norms of residence rights being obtained through ownership of coconut trees and descent group membership.

TABLE II

Methods of obtaining coconut trees in Minazini

	1 Bought	2 Inherited	3 Planted	4 Other	5 Total
Men	4,023	7,613	3,719	1,086	16,441
Women	182	3,192	300	128	3,802
Total	4,205	10,805	4,019	1,214	20,243

Notes: Column 2 (inherited). Women owners average 30 trees inherited, while men average 45. This is a higher proportion than might be expected at the 2:1 rate of inheritance, and is explained by the greater reluctance of women to part with their trees; the fact that women inherit more often from their husbands than the other way round; and, finally, that women receive *mahari* from their husbands (this is included as inheritance).

Column 3 (planted). Women probably own more of the planted trees than these figures indicate. When a husband and wife plant a field together, the trees are usually in the husband's name, and it is only after his death that the wife claims her share.

Column 4 (other). This column includes trees acquired by gift, renting, and those trees held under *wakf* or *shirika*.

Factors involved in residence decisions

Taking the ownership of coconut trees and membership in a descent group as the criteria for conferring residence rights in a ward, it may be asked to what extent people have a choice about where to reside. Many men in the village are members of more than one descent group, but only ten own trees in more than one ward associated with descent groups of which they are members.

What are the factors which contribute to this state of affairs? One explanation is that, if a sibling group inherits trees in a number of wards, it may split up, with each brother taking trees in different areas. This had happened to two men who inherited trees from their father on land of groups D and E. They split the inheritance, with each man taking a grove in a different ward.

Another reason is that husbands and wives often own trees in the same ward so that their children inherit trees in one ward only. This may be either because of the high rate of intra-descent group marriage or because a couple planted trees together in the same ward.

Finally, it must be remembered that some women never acquire any trees at all, hence children inherit only from their fathers. Or, if a husband dies first, his wife inherits along with their children, and then her share eventually passes to them.

Another explanation of why men tend to own trees in only one ward is that they may well sell trees if they inherit them in several areas. People prefer to reside near to their trees, so that they can keep an eye on them; and of course, it is easier to fell the nuts in a single grove than in several scattered holdings.

Now the main method of acquiring trees, as I have already shown, is through inheritance. Since men obviously own more trees than women, it might be expected that men would tend to inherit more from their fathers than their mothers, and thus be more likely to settle in the wards of the former. At first sight, this would seem to be the case; men do inherit trees more often and in greater quantities from their fathers than from their mothers. Furthermore, for those men who do not own trees, it is necessary, should they live on ward land, to live with a relative who does own trees, and the most obvious choice is the father, as Table 12 shows.

TABLE 12
Residence and coconut trees

	No. of men	%
Resident in coconut groves inherited from:		
Father	49	(23%)
Mother	19	(9%)
Father and mother	11	(5%)
Other	6	(3%)
Resident in coconut groves owned by:		
Father	23	(11%)
Mother	13	(6%)
Other relative	5	(2%)
Affines (including wife)	9	(4%)
Other and unknown	17	(9%)
Resident in coconut groves acquired by:		
Buying	34	(16%)
Planting	24	(11%)
	210	(100%)

Table 12 shows that a far higher proportion of men reside on land they have inherited from their fathers than from their mothers, and also more reside on coconut groves owned by their fathers than their mothers. Furthermore, since virilocality is the norm of residence after marriage, it might be expected that all men would be brought up in their fathers' wards, and so choose to live there, thus further increasing the bias towards the male line already caused by inheritance. But if we look at residence from the point of view of descent group membership, in fact we find that patrilocality is not the statistical norm. Almost as many men live in the wards of their mothers' descent groups as in those of their fathers', and a considerable number live in wards associated with both parents (i.e. they are the children of an intra-descent group marriage), as Table 13 shows.

TABLE 13*

Choice of residence with reference to the descent groups of father and mother

		Number	%
Men residing in fathers' wards †		55	30
„ „ mothers' wards		42	22
„ „ fathers' and mothers' wards		38	20
„ „ elsewhere ‡		52	28
Totals		187	100

Notes:

* This table considers only those men who have membership of a Minazini descent group.

† i.e. wards, rights to which were acquired through membership of fathers' descent groups—not necessarily wards in which fathers themselves actually resided.

‡ This figure includes men residing on non-ward land, and also men residing on ward land held by groups of which they are not members.

Tables 12 and 13, then, reveal an apparent contradiction. Nearly a quarter of all men are resident on coconut groves which they have inherited from their fathers, in comparison with only 9 per cent residing on the groves inherited from their mothers. Men who own no trees are more likely to use their fathers' groves to obtain residence rights (11 per cent) than their mothers' groves (6 per cent). Yet if we ask whether a man is more likely to reside in the ward associated with the descent group of his father or mother, we find that the discrepancies are not nearly as great; while 30 per cent of men reside with their fathers' descent groups, 22 per cent of men reside with those of their mothers', and a further 20 per cent reside in wards associated with a descent group of both parents.

The explanation which reconciles this apparent contradiction is that many men have acquired trees in their mothers' wards by buying and planting, and the question which then arises is why men so desire to live in their mothers' wards that they go to the trouble of acquiring trees there. In order to understand more fully the reasons for residence choices it is necessary to consider the composition of small units within the wards—households and clusters.

The household

The household is defined as the primary unit of production and consumption, and it may be composed of one or more houses. The great majority of households are made up of a husband and wife and their young children, i.e. they are nuclear, but a few also contain an elderly relative, or a divorced or widowed younger woman with her children. Although polygyny is permitted under Islamic law, only a minority of men in Minazini (10 per cent) have more than one wife, and all of these wives live in separate households.

Table 14 gives the composition of households in Minazini.

TABLE 14
Household composition

				No.	
Nuclear family				181	(67%)
,,	,,	+ aged relative		6	(2%)
,,	,,	+ relatives' children		15	(5%)
,,	,,	+ grandchildren		24	(9%)
Men living alone				13	(5%)
Women living alone				5	(2%)
,,	,,	with own children		6	(2%)
,,	,,	,,	sisters	3	(1%)
,,	,,	,,	mothers	5	(2%)
,,	,,	,,	relatives' children	13	(5%)
Total households				271	(100%)

As Table 14 shows, there is a total of 271 households in Minazini and thus the average size of a household is 3·5 persons.

It is noticeable that only a few aged parents are living with their children. Normally old people remain independent for as long as possible, and continue to cultivate their own fields, and cook for themselves. It is only when a man or woman is left alone, and not always then, that he or she decides to go and live with a child. Even so, a separate house is always built, and an attempt made to cultivate a separate field, right up to the time of chronic sickness, senility or death.

The table also draws attention to the number of households (nearly

20 per cent) which contain children other than those of the husband or wife. This is because of a system of 'fostering' (*ulezi*), whereby a child is sent, either temporarily or permanently, to be brought up by a relative, usually a grandparent, or the sibling of one of its parents. Approximately 25 per cent of the children in Minazini are being fostered in this way.[3] There are various reasons for this custom. One of the most important is economic. Even in a good year, as already pointed out in Chapter 1, it is probable that many households in Minazini live below what the people themselves consider to be a decent standard. Those with large numbers of children may be glad to foster some of them out. Normally such children are taken by grandparents who no longer have any children living at home, or by childless siblings of the parents. The couple who undertake the fostering of a child are responsible for its food and clothing for as long as it is under their roof, although occasionally the parents may send a small gift, if they can afford to do so.

But reasons for fostering are not only economic. Grandparents say that they are lonely when all their children have left home, and they are impatient for the arrival of grandchildren. It is sometimes said that grandparents have greater rights over children than do parents, and this applies particularly to the grandparent after whom the child was named; each refers to the other as *somo*. This relationship was mentioned a number of times to me; once a child cut his mouth when he fell off my Land-Rover, but the parents themselves refused to discuss the matter with me, saying it was the responsibility of the boy's *somo* grandfather. On another occasion I asked a man jokingly if I could take his child back to England with me to study; he replied seriously that such a decision could only be made by his *somo* grandfather.

The relationship between grandparents and grandchildren is not an authoritarian one—on the contrary, they have an institutionalized joking relationship (*utani*).[4] This indeed may be one reason why grandparents welcome their grandchildren to bring up—they do not need to maintain as formal a relationship with them as they did with their own children. In addition, having brought up a family of their own, they are less worried about the children, and the relationship is characterized by easy familiarity, and frequent teasing.

It should be noted that women are married as soon as they reach puberty, so that many of them become mothers when very young. People say that they 'know nothing', and that they are incapable of bringing up children, since they are still children themselves. Thus it is better that children should be in the hands of someone experienced. Mothers themselves may agree. One girl said to me: 'When I had my first baby I was 15, and I didn't even know how to carry it on my back!' Some girls quickly become pregnant again, and are glad to hand over the care of their first child to their mothers.

Another reason why it is often necessary to hand over a child to a relative is divorce which has already been shown to be common in Minazini. Divorced women often find it impossible to maintain themselves and their children, as their ex-husbands pay them no maintenance. A young woman is unlikely to have any source of income, except from the field she cultivates, and perhaps from plaiting a few mats. Her mother, on the other hand, as an older woman, will usually own a few coconut trees, which she has inherited from either parents or husbands, and in addition, if she has been widowed or divorced more than once, she will have received marriage payments. Thus her economic position will be much stronger than that of her divorced daughter, and this is the reason why even older women living alone are able to afford the burden of caring for the children of relatives.

Sometimes children go to live with a relative temporarily. Thus a divorced woman may hand over her child to her mother from the time of her divorce, until she is re-married and settled in her new home. Other children go to stay with a relative merely to 'visit' (*matembezi*). One old woman whose house was next to mine never had the same children in her household two weeks running—she was constantly invaded by her different grandchildren.

Children thus serve as a link between relatives who are otherwise dispersed, although not all of the relatives with whom children are fostered out necessarily live far away; they may even be neighbours. When children stay for a long time away from their parents, they are visited by them, and of course they know who their parents are. They retain all the rights of a child, particularly with regard to inheritance, and the parents likewise retain the duty to see that they have a proper puberty ceremony, and are married off to suitable people.

Children, then, may grow up in a number of households, even in a number of villages. Although most of their rights are vested with their parents, long residence in childhood with another relative may influence a man in his choice of where to reside, so that he settles near to his relative, rather than near to his parents. A foster child may even be given the gift of a few trees, although he or she would never inherit from a foster-parent. However, gifts are rare, unless the foster-parent has no children, and so foster-children who wish to settle near their foster-parents would have to buy or plant trees.

The cluster

A cluster is a group of households in close proximity, separated from other neighbouring domestic groups whose occupants are close kin. There are forty-two such clusters in Minazini, and half of the houses in the village form part of a cluster. The average number of households per cluster is three. Clusters may be categorized into several types, but usually there is a focal household having a male at its head. Other households are grouped around this focal unit. A few clusters consist of polygynously married men and their wives, although most co-wives reside in separate clusters. Other clusters contain divorced sisters, daughters and mothers of focal household heads; unmarried women rarely live completely alone, as in many situations women need a man's help.

It is rather difficult to give statistics of cluster composition, as the number of permutations is much greater than for households. However the following table gives some idea of the frequency with which certain combinations of relatives occur:

TABLE 15
Cluster composition

	No.	
Male siblings	16	38%
Father and sons	19	45%
Father and (divorced) daughters	7	17%
Brothers and (divorced) sisters	5	12%
Mothers (divorced) and sons	10	24%
Others	11	26%

Note: These categories are not exclusive—some clusters contain more than one combination of relatives.

As can be seen, the commonest combination of kinsmen is fathers and sons, closely followed by male siblings. However, it should be noted that male siblings rarely stay together after the death of their father, or in some instances, father's brother. In other words, normally men accept the leadership of a cluster head provided that he is of a senior generation.

The following genealogy illustrates the composition of a cluster which contains both a father and his sons, and a pair of male siblings who are the FBS of the cluster head, and their married sister.

This cluster consists of seven households—W.A.'s two wives each have a separate household. All except the household of A.M. consist of one house only; A.M.'s son, a boy of about 12 years, has recently moved out of his parents' house and has built a hut alongside—a normal practice for boys when they reach puberty.

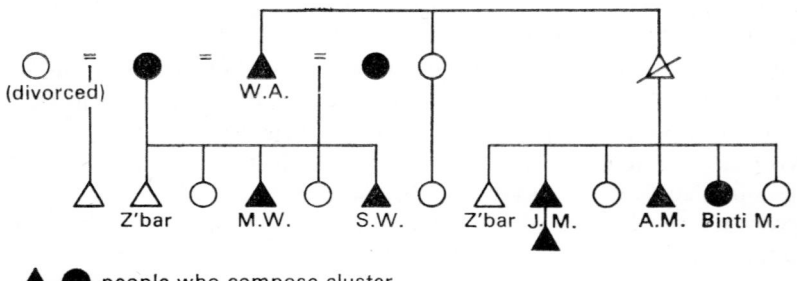

people who compose cluster

FIG. 5

Composition of a cluster (example)

The cluster is thus part of a small segment (*tumbo*). However, the segment is not complete. W.A.'s eldest son, by a woman he divorced some time ago, lives in a village in central Mafia. He is not on good terms with his father, probably because of his mother's divorce. W.A.'s second son and one of his brother's sons live in Zanzibar, and have been there for a number of years. Five of his six daughters are married out of the cluster.

Why do these people live in the same cluster? There are three sorts of reasons which can be distinguished. The first is that people in a cluster may all have their coconut trees there, and this gives them residential rights. Or, if they have no trees, they are forced to live with a kinsman who does. Not only do coconut trees confer residential rights, but for practical reasons people like to be near trees which they can use daily—to fell nuts for cooking, to obtain palm fronds for fuel, and for repairing roofs, making baskets, etc. In W.A.'s cluster, his two sons live near to him because they have no trees of their own, and their only alternative would be to live on non-ward land.

A second reason is that men are attracted by the cluster leader, particularly if he has wealth, and prestige. In this instance, W.A. is a wealthy man, by Minazini standards; he is also a spirit shaman. His two sons depend upon him for economic support occasionally; in fact one of them is tubercular, and cannot cultivate very much. All the men of the younger generation defer to W.A. Thus, for example, when W.A. quarrelled with a near kinsman, they followed him in refusing a reconciliation, even though one of them privately told me that they thought the quarrel was about a trifling matter.

In W.A.'s cluster, J.M. and his brother A.M. have no need to stay living with W.A. since they both own coconut fields elsewhere in the village, and in a neighbouring village too. However, their parents both lived in this cluster, and were buried there, and both the brothers grew up there. J.M. may have a more positive reason for staying: he often acts as the cluster representative, since W.A. is now very old. Perhaps he hopes to take over leadership of the cluster, and indeed, since J.M. is a successful trader, and is much respected for his piety and learning, this is quite possible. At least he is certain that his younger brother A.M. will remain with him, since the latter has six children, and is very poor, while J.M. has no children, and frequently helps his brother economically.

A third factor is that clusters are held together by their common interest in the grave sites attached to them. More than anything else, the grave site symbolizes the fact that this is 'home' (*kwetu*); if a man's father or mother are buried in a particular cluster, then a child too has a right to be buried there. Furthermore, a number of kinship rituals are focused on the graves of ancestors. In the seventh month of the Islamic calendar, graves are swept, and a Koranic reading is held to ask forgiveness for sins (*kuarehemu wazee*). In addition, many men and women hold special Koranic readings on the anniversary of a parent's death (*hitima ya mwanasha*).

If the father and mother are buried in different clusters, then both will be 'home' in this ritual sense for their children, and will be equally attended for ritual purposes. Thus even for those who do not reside in a particular cluster, emotional ties remain, and the cluster serves as a focus for the dispersed ritual unit. As a residential unit, a cluster need not consist of more than one household. Sometimes, at a particular stage in the 'developmental cycle' of a cluster—as for example at the death of a father, and the dispersion of children—only one remains in the cluster. But the other children still look to the cluster as a focus, and refer to it as 'our place' (*mji wetu*). This is true in the case of W.A.'s cluster; the remainder of his children and the children of his brother return to this cluster on ritual occasions.

Finally, a factor which operates in some cases is that, in addition to holding coconut trees in a particular place, a man also owns a fairly substantial house there. There are two main types of houses in Minazini—huts built of palm thatch, which can be quickly erected, and houses built of mangrove poles and mud. The latter can vary considerably in size, but a large and well-built one will last for many years. If a man inherits a house of this type, he is likely to move into it. Similarly, if he himself manages to build such a house, he is unlikely to want to move away and leave it. Most older men aim at acquiring a fairly large house, which means that they are not very mobile, while most younger men live in more flimsy structures, which can easily be abandoned. Thus J.M. in W.A.'s cluster is building himself a large house, which really means that he has made his residential decision, and is unlikely to move from this cluster and ward.

Although marriage is normally virilocal, in W.A.'s cluster one woman has remained with her kin, instead of living with her husband's kin. It is quite likely that her sons, when they become adult, will choose to continue to live in this cluster, which means that they will be living in their mother's ward. This is not an isolated instance, as the following case history shows:

CASE 3

The residence patterns of Binti M. and her children

Binti M. is about 60 years of age. She was born in a village near to Minazini (I shall refer to it as X) where her mother's mother was living at the time. After the birth (for which, as is customary, Binti M.'s mother returned to her own mother), Binti M.'s mother returned to her husband, i.e. Binti M.'s father in Baleni village in central Mafia. Binti M. remained in Baleni village with her mother and father until they divorced, and she then went with her mother back to X village in the north of the Island.

At puberty, Binti M. married a Minazini man, and she bore him one son before she was divorced, and returned to her mother in X village. This son, when he grew up, lived with his father in cluster I (cf. Fig. 6).

Binti M. re-married, again to a Minazini man, and she bore him four sons before his death.

Her third marriage was also to a Minazini man, although by this time she was past the age of child bearing. She was living with this husband in his cluster (IV) at the time of the study (1966), but he died soon afterwards. Binti M. is now unlikely to re-marry, so that her choice of residence is not affected by where her husband is living, but rather by the whereabouts of her children.

Binti M.'s five sons live as follows:

The eldest, by her first husband, lives in Minazini in the cluster where his father lived (cluster I). This son inherited trees there. He died in 1966, and was buried in this cluster. His eldest son, who was already married and living with his two wives in the same cluster as his father, then assumed leadership of the cluster. His widowed mother, and a divorced sister continued to live in this same cluster (I).

Binti M.'s second son (by her second marriage) lives in Tumbuju village, in an area in central Mafia which is newly opened up, and immigrants from many parts of the island, and even from the mainland, have settled there in order to plant coconut trees, since there is a large amount of land available, and the soil is suited to coconut trees. This man originally lived in cluster II, where his father had also lived, and in fact he still has a house and some coconut trees there.

The third son lives in X village, in his mother's mother's cluster (III). He was brought up there, and his mother's sister lives in the same cluster. Since his mother owns coconut trees there, he is likely to acquire trees by inheritance from her, but in any case he has already been able to acquire trees there by buying or planting. If he decides to live in this cluster permanently, he may well exchange some of his Minazini trees with his brothers for their share of the X village inheritance, so that all his trees will be in this one cluster in X. On the other hand, he may decide to retain his Minazini trees, as this gives him the right to go and live there at any time.

The fourth and fifth sons both live in Minazini in the cluster (II) where their father had lived. However, the younger of the two brothers has recently purchased coconut trees on the outskirts of the village, and talks of moving there as soon as possible. This would leave only one son in his father's cluster.

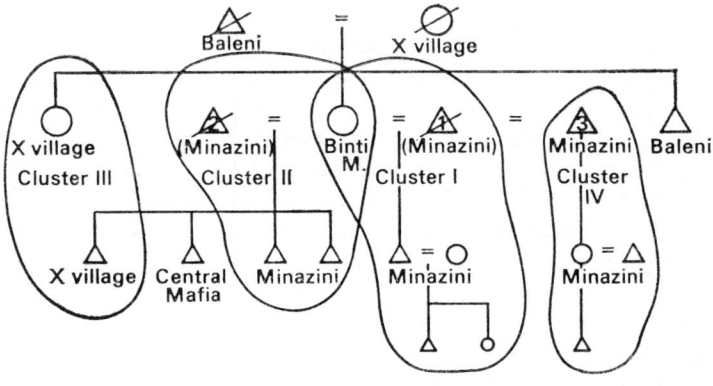

FIG. 6

Composition and formation of clusters: Binti M. and her children

Thus, after the death of her third husband, Binti M. has the following possibilities open to her:

(a) to live in the cluster (II) of her sons in Minazini.

(b) to live in the cluster of her son's son (I), also in Minazini.

(c) to live in the cluster of her elder sister and son in X village where she herself owns coconut trees (III).

(d) to remain in the cluster (IV) where she was living with her last husband. Although she will inherit trees there, she is unlikely to stay there, since the other cluster IV members are a daughter of her late husband by a previous marriage and this woman's husband and son.

(e) to go and live with her elder brother in Baleni. In this particular case, it is extremely unlikely, as she quarrelled with him many years ago over her portion of their inheritance in Baleni, and she has been unable to establish claims over any coconut trees there.

The main factors in such a choice are, first of all, the emotional pull of 'home', which in this case is the X village cluster where she spent her girlhood (i.e. cluster III), secondly, the fact that she has lived nearly all her adult life in Minazini, thirdly, the whereabouts of her near relatives, particularly sons and siblings, and finally, the whereabouts of her coconut trees.

Binti M. finally went to live in cluster II where her two youngest sons were living.

This case history illustrates likely residence patterns of both men and women. For the latter, choice is mainly, although not always, dictated by the man they marry, but when divorced or widowed women do have a choice about where they will live. Usually even then their choice is limited by the ideal that they should reside with a male relative, since, under Islamic law, an unmarried woman is always under the guardianship of either her father, brother, or even son. In purely practical terms, most single women are forced to live in the cluster of a male relative, since if they are young and own no coconut trees they need some kind of economic help, and even if they do own trees they usually need a man's help in arranging for the nuts to be felled and marketed. Those women who do not have any rights in meadow fields also need a man's help in cultivating a bush field. Thus the great majority of women living alone or with children (cf. Table 14) are nearly all living in the same cluster, although not the same household, as a male relative.

Men's residence, on the other hand, is rarely affected by marriage, since only a handful live uxorilocally. The ownership of coconut trees is important but not the sole deciding factor. Thus Binti M.'s third son lives in his mother's mother's cluster in X village largely because he spent much of his childhood there. Whether or not brothers remain together in a cluster depends to a large extent upon there being a focus, i.e. a cluster leader. Thus the cluster formerly made up of the three younger sons of Binti M. by her second marriage is breaking up, because none of the brothers is sufficiently wealthy or prestigious to encourage the others to accept his leadership.

It may well be that soon there will only be one household left in this cluster. However, it will still serve as a focus for the dispersed sibling group since the members will have an interest in the trees and graves there, and a new cluster may form around the remaining son when his own children are adult. Had there been any sisters in this sibling group, they might have returned, after divorce or widowhood, to live in their brother's cluster, and perhaps their children might also have chosen to live there when adult. Thus cluster formation has to be viewed over a period of time. An examination of those households which form part of a cluster and those which do not often reveals that they are at different stages in their developmental cycle.

Conclusion

Residence patterns can be viewed in a number of ways. People say that they have a right to reside on land where they own trees. This, given the fact that men get more trees from their fathers than their mothers, would militate towards patrilocality, and the norm of post-marital virilocality would also seem to reinforce this tendency.

TABLE 16
Male members residing with their descent groups

Name of group	% of male members residing
A	61
B	31
C	18
D	36
E	55
F	66

On the other hand many men do receive trees from their mothers, and, given the high rates of divorce and fostering, may have grown up among their mothers' kin, so choosing to live with them rather than the fathers' kin.

Thus people do not make their residential choices primarily in terms of their membership of descent groups. Since most land on which coconuts have been planted is also descent group land, and since people are discouraged from selling trees to those who are not members of the same group, few people acquire trees on ward land where they do not have descent group membership already. The handful of people who do acquire trees elsewhere do not usually take up the residential rights thereby conferred.

Finally, we may ask what is the outcome of all these individual choices—are people distributed more or less at random among the wards of the six descent groups, or do some groups have a higher proportion of their members residing in their wards than do others?

Three descent groups (A, E and F) have a majority of their male members residing in their wards. The remaining three descent groups attract a much smaller proportion of members to their wards. One of the questions to be asked in the rest of this book is whether these proportions remain constant in other contexts of affiliation. And, if they do, can it then be argued that choice of residence thus influences choices in other contexts, even that residence is, in effect, a 'closing' factor in descent group membership?

CHAPTER 4

LAND TENURE[1]

Categories of cultivable land

In Chapter 1 I noted that the two most important types of cultivable land in Minazini are bush land and meadow[2] land. The former lies outside the village, mainly on higher ground, and supports a variety of crops including hill rice, corn, millet, beans, and pumpkins. The latter, which is situated within the village wards, is low-lying and therefore flooded during the wet season; here only rice and sweet potatoes are grown, and coconut trees planted. While bush land can be cultivated for only a short period, and then must lie fallow, meadows can be cultivated on a semi-permanent basis. Bush land is cultivated on a five-year cycle; after a year's cultivation, it is left fallow for four years. Rights to bush and meadow land are obtained through descent group membership, but each type of land is associated with a somewhat different system of holding, and the two will therefore be dealt with separately in this chapter.

In addition to bush and meadow land there is also a large area of fertile land set aside for the growing of cassava. This is a recent development, initiated by the agriculture department. Government officials were anxious to promote cultivation on a communal basis, but the villagers strongly resisted the idea, and eventually the land was divided into individual fields allocated by the District Agricultural Officer. Rights to this land are not obtained through descent group membership; any member of the village can obtain a plot of land, and there is plenty of room for expansion. By 1967 nearly 100 fields were being cultivated in this area.

The cassava area is not discussed in any detail, as rights to it are not concerned with descent. However, it does highlight the variance between the government's attitude to land and that of the villagers. Originally the cassava area was part of the bush held by descent groups. Only members had rights to this land; other people had to ask their permission. However, the government does not recognize that land may be held by descent groups or individuals. The right of free-hold[3] has been abolished in Tanzania since Independence and all lands declared government property. Any individual may take up a piece of unused land and cultivate it. Thus the Agricultural Officer, having decided that the soil was suitable in this area, encouraged the planting of cassava on a large scale, regardless of the fact that this land was claimed by members of a descent group.

The only type of land which the government recognizes as capable of being held by an individual or a group is that on which certain trees —principally coconut, cashewnut, and mango trees—are growing. The trees on such land may be bought, sold, inherited, leased, given as a gift, etc. But in the eyes of the government, the only method of acquiring any sort of rights over other types of land is to cultivate crops, which confers only temporary rights, or to plant trees, which confers permanent rights.

This conflict between village custom and government law which can not only be enforced in the courts, but also is usually enforced by the Village Development Council (VDC), is deplored by most of the villagers. However a small number of villagers are beginning to use government law as an excuse for obtaining land which was previously not available to them; as will be seen, many disputes over land arise out of this conflict.

Bush land

Bush land may be subdivided into two types—that which is and is not associated with descent groups. Some mention of the latter was made in the last chapter when discussing the 'new areas' (i.e. non-ward land) on the outskirts of the village, particularly to the north and east, where people cultivate annual crops, and in addition are planting coconut trees and establishing permanent rights. This type of bush, where anyone may take up land, is only a small part of the total bush area.

Most of the bush land, as has already been stated, is held by descent groups and most people have to obtain rights by virtue of their membership of descent groups. Some villagers are also able to obtain rights to land in neighbouring villages, if they are members of descent groups there.

Both men and women have equal rights in the land of their descent groups. Only one field is usually cultivated by a married couple in any one year; thus the couple can choose whether to obtain their rights through the husband's descent group, or the wife's, or by some other means.

Bush land is plentiful in Minazini. However, not all descent groups have the same amount of bush at their disposal. Descent group C has no bush land at all, while descent group F holds nearly 70 per cent of all bush land associated with descent groups. This means that people who do not belong to group F but who wish to cultivate bush land have to get F group land through other ties, as will be shown.

The following table shows the amount of bush land available in any one year, and its distribution among the descent groups.

TABLE 17
Distribution of bush land *

Descent group	No. of members† able to claim land in one year	No. of fields available in one year‡	Approx. ratio of members to fields
A	38	5 (3%)	7:1
B	62	18 (10%)	4:1
C	29	0	—
D	53	15 (9%)	3:1
E	42	21 (11·5%)	2:1
F	111	127 (69%)	1:1

Notes:

* These figures were obtained mainly from informants, chiefly the Elders of the descent groups concerned, or the F group Guardians (see below). It was quite impossible to count or measure all the fields, which cover over 2,500 acres. Informants said how many fields were available in any particular area, and by a 'field' they said they meant what a couple usually cultivated—that is between 2½ and 3 acres (cf. Chapter 1).

† For the purposes of this table, I have halved the total number of members of each descent group, since it would have included both men and women, and thus given an entirely unrealistic ratio. Fields are normally cultivated by a married couple, and it is rare for them to cultivate more than one field, certainly never more than one bush field (except for polygynously married men) in a single year.

‡ After obtaining the estimate of the total number of fields (as defined above) from informants, I then divided this by five, to give the number available in any one year, since bush fields are cultivated one year in five. Inevitably, this is something of an over-simplification, because slightly more fields may be available in one year than another; thus the figures in column 3 represent an average.

In all 183 bush fields are thus available in any one year, in addition to those in the new areas not included in Table 17. Since, however, there are some 276 women and 210 men in the village, it is obvious that not all of them can cultivate a bush field. Many do not wish to do so, particularly single men or women, and older people, because the work is much harder than cultivating meadow land. On the whole, younger couples prefer bush land, because they can obtain such a wide variety of crops. Some people also prefer bush fields because the crops ripen earlier. Thus in 1966 145 bush fields were cultivated by Minazini villagers—not as many as were available. Not all of these fields were associated with Minazini descent groups; seventeen of them in fact belonged to neighbouring villages, and a further 21 were non-ward land (cf. Chapter 3). Thus only 107 bush fields associated with descent groups, out of the 183 available, were actually used in 1966, as the following table shows:

TABLE 18
Bush land cultivated in 1966

Descent group with which land associated	No. of fields cultivated	No. of fields available
A	8	5*
B	7	18
C	0	0
D	8	15
E	8	21
F	76	127

Note:
* The discrepancy between the A group figures is explained by the fact that the number of fields given as available for one year is an average; in any case, in 1966 two of the A group's fields were being cultivated by elderly, single people, who could only manage very small areas of land.

In the case of every descent group except group A, which appeared to cultivate all the bush land it had available, and group C, which in any case possesses no bush land, all the descent groups cultivated less land than was available. The main reason for this is, of course, that many of the people who are entitled to claim bush land do not do so, as they prefer to cultivate meadow land. For this reason people say 'a man should have as much (bush) land as he can cultivate'.

How bush land is allocated—primary right holders

Three types of holders of bush land may be distinguished—primary, secondary, and tertiary.[4] They are defined in the course of this section.

Bush land, as has already been stated, is associated with descent groups. However the large named areas held by the descent groups are subdivided into smaller sections, known as *mavumvu*, which are held by segments of the descent groups. Minazini people explain this by saying that a man or woman some time in the past acquired primary rights over this section of bush, by either clearing it or buying it (as was formerly possible), or else by being made a gift of it. These rights were inherited by his or her descendants, both male and female.

An example of the way in which bush land is divided between segments of a descent group is given in Fig. 7. This is a much simplified genealogy of the B descent group. Sections of land are held by the large segments (a + b); these are in this particular case segments which also hold the two B group wards. The segment holding the northern ward (*a*) is the primary holder of a section called Kunde, while the segment (*b*) which resides in the southern ward cultivates Omazi and Schuali land. Both of these segments however (that is, all the B descent group members) may cultivate Upeko section land. The smaller segments shown on the genealogy are not as significant in land holding, although the Elder of each of the smaller segments has a say in the allocation of the land of the larger segment to which he belongs.

Primary right holders, then, are members of a segment holding a section of bush land. All members of the segment have a right to some land of their section. The process of allocation is quite informal, unless there is a localized shortage. Normally, every year, just before the opening of the cultivation season in November, the men of the village are to be seen sitting round in little groups, and the main topic of conversation is where each will cultivate the following season. Each primary right holder states his preferences, and mentions them to other members of the segment holding the section he wants to cultivate. Provided that no one else claims that particular piece of land, he then goes off to the field he has chosen, and makes some cuts on some of the trees growing there. This signifies his intention to cut down the bush in that field, and cultivate it. After this is done, no man should interfere with that field.

This was a norm accepted by all the villagers until very recently. However, as the following case shows, it is no longer enforced by the Village Development Committee, and some villagers can use the government law to justify their cultivation of land which has already been 'spoken for'.

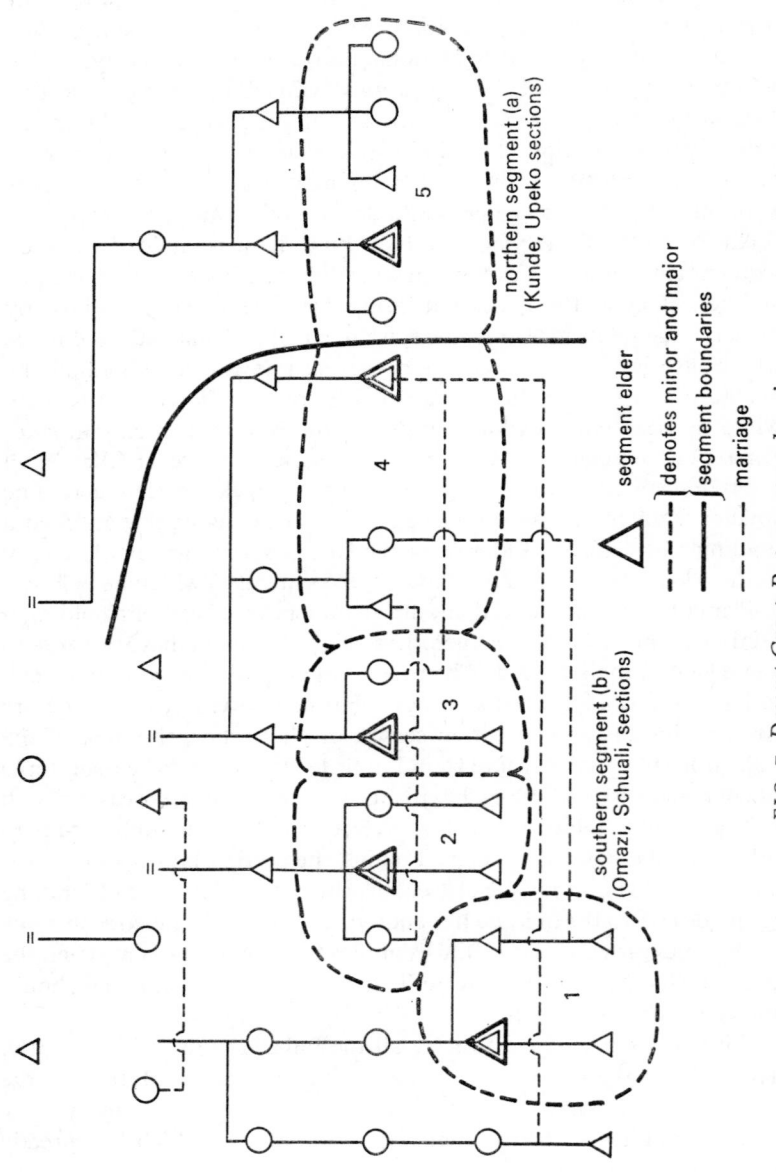

FIG. 7 *Descent Group B: segments and sections*

northern segment (a)
(Kunde, Upeko sections)

southern segment (b)
(Omazi, Schuali, sections)

segment elder

} denotes minor and major
} segment boundaries

marriage

CASE 4

Dispute over fields

Athman, an old man of descent group F, wished to obtain three fields in the 1966–7 season, one to cultivate himself, another for his son, and a third for his daughter and her husband.

During the discussions in October 1966, he stated which three fields he wanted to take. However, when he went to one of the fields (field 1), he found that another man of his segment, Seleman, had already started to cultivate there. Athman was annoyed, but decided to let the matter drop, as he had not in fact marked the field by blazing some trees.

He went off and marked two other fields (2 and 3), and told his son-in-law that he would have to look elsewhere. Soon afterwards, however, the same man who had taken his field 1, also came and started to cultivate in field 2, claiming that he needed two fields, one for himself and his wife, and one for his divorced sister.

Athman decided that he had a case against Seleman, and took him before the VDC. However, the Council maintained that under government law it could do nothing, as Athman had not actually started to cultivate the field. The VDC suggested a compromise measure whereby field 2 should be divided equally between the disputants.

Athman felt, as did my informant on this case (it happened while I was away from the village) that the second man had no right to take land which had already been marked by him.[5] The VDC, on the other hand, adhered to its interpretation of government law which says that any man may cultivate unused bush, regardless of his status.

Athman's case was strengthened by the fact that the other people, for whom he was obtaining the land, were people with primary rights. His own son was, of course, a segment member, and so was his daughter. Daughters retain full rights over their segment land, even when they are married away. Normally, however, a son-in-law will come and ask his wife's father's permission to cultivate, rather than assume that he has a right. Single daughters are quite entitled to land of their segments. If, however, Athman had wanted to take land for other relatives or affines who did not have such a strong claim as his son or his daughter and her husband, then the other man would have been quite justified in opposing him, and claiming that he had a better right to the land. In other words, primary right-holders have first claim on land.

This case shows that disputes do sometimes arise because of localized shortages of land. One man explained it in this way: 'Perhaps our section only takes five people, and there are seven of us (wanting to get land there). Either we will agree to take smaller fields that year, or else two of us won't get land (in that section) and will go elsewhere. Another year those people will have priority, because they missed out before.' Such matters can usually be settled quite amicably, because nearly everyone has several options about where he can cultivate.

When disputes do become serious, there are two courses open to the contenders: the one is to take the case before the VDC, as Athman did, the other is to consult one of the Elders of a descent group (each one of whom is normally a segment leader), or, where F group land is involved, to consult a Guardian (their roles are discussed below). As already mentioned in Chapter 2, Elderhood is not a formal office, but certain old men who are recognized as repositories of genealogical knowledge are in a position to say who may or may not cultivate land. (Elders of the B descent group are shown on the genealogy, Fig. 7.)

Elders make it their business to know who proposes to cultivate where in any particular season, so that they will know whether or not there is land to spare for non-primary right-holders. In the case of primary right-holders, they will recall which of the members of the segment had priority the previous year and make sure that someone else gets a turn. One man said to me in 1966: 'I wanted to cultivate the land of my D group segment again this year but the Elder of my segment said to me "you cultivated last year with us; this year you must get land elsewhere". So I didn't get land with that segment, but cultivated with my wife's D group segment.'

On F group land, the situation is somewhat different. The Elders have little say in the allocation of land. Instead, there are Guardians of spirit shrines, which are scattered over the F group's bush. The spirits (*mizimu*) are said to own and guard the land; indeed they are usually referred to as the '*Wazee*' (elders) as a term of respect, denoting their rights over this land. (It should be noted that spirits are not associated with the land of other descent groups.) The Guardians, who are spirit shamans (cf. Chapter 6) lead the propitiatory rites which are held at three crucial stages in the agricultural cycle—when the bush is cut down, at the beginning of the harvest, and at the very end when all the cultivators have moved back to their houses in the village and abandoned their fields.

There are four shrines, and four Guardians. A small part of group F's land, however, is not considered to be ruled over by a spirit, and no rites are held on this land. Even there, however, two of the Guardians have the power to allocate land.

People often validate their rights to land not so much in terms of descent as of kinship to the Elder of a segment, or one of the F group Guardians, as in the following case:

CASE 5

Dispute over an F group field

Silima and Ali both wanted to cultivate the same field on group F's land. They were both members of the same segment. They went to an Elder of the descent group, and asked him which had the better right. He replied that Silima had, because he was more closely related to one of the Guardians.

The Elder went on to add that no one who was not related to a Guardian could get F group's land.

Genealogical enquiry proved that in fact Ali had the better right, since he was much more closely related to the Guardian in question, and that if a descent, rather than a kinship framework were used, Ali would still have a stronger claim, because two of his grandparents were members of the segment, whereas only one of Silima's was, as the following genealogy shows:

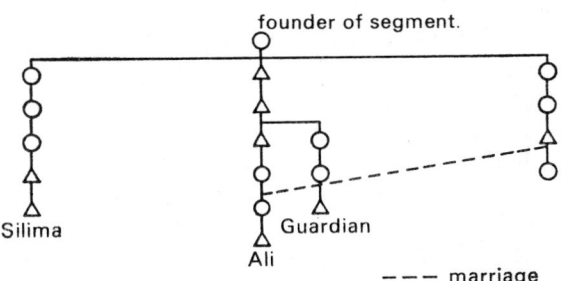

FIG. 8

Dispute over an F group field: relationship between Guardian and disputants

This case also illustrates the power that Elders can wield, because of their genealogical knowledge—they can, and do, in fact, manipulate genealogies. The Elder in this case may have had specific reasons for wishing to favour Silima, since they were both members of the same spirit possession guild.

The Guardians of F group land have more power than the Elders of the other descent groups, because they act as intermediaries with the spirits. While people are living out in the G group's fields for four to five months, they have to observe certain strict rules of behaviour, and in particular to maintain a high standard of personal hygiene. It is thought that the spirits most dislike 'dirt' and quarrelling. Thus people who fail to wash after intercourse or who have an argument with neighbours will incur the wrath of the spirit who is the ruler of their fields, and are thought likely to become very sick. The Guardians can use the threat of mystical retribution to oblige people to behave properly, and not to quarrel over land.

All people who cultivate F group fields contribute to the offerings made to the spirit of the field, regardless of whether they are themselves F group members or outsiders who have obtained the land by other links (i.e. tertiary right-holders, who are discussed below). Thus even the Imam of the mosque, who, after the Sheikh, is considered to be the most pious person in the village, on several occasions has cultivated F group land, and contributed to the offerings to the spirits, although orthodox Islam considers this is quite unlawful (*haramu*). It is said that the spirits will not guard the fields of those who do not make the requisite offerings.

Occasionally, it is argued that an F group spirit may extend its protection to a neighbouring field belonging to a different descent group. One man who cultivated a D group field, to which his descent did not entitle him, made offerings to the spirit of the neighbouring F group field, along with other F group people. Later a large baobab tree fell down and destroyed part of his crop. I asked one informant if it would be considered that the D group people who opposed his cultivating this field had caused this to happen to punish him for taking the field without permission. My informant replied that there was no possibility of anyone practising witchcraft in that field, since the cultivator had placed it under the protection of a spirit (cf. Case 6).

Non-primary right-holders

I have thus far been discussing people with primary rights to land, i.e. rights over a section of bush land associated with the descent group segment of which they are members. Secondary right-holders are people who are members of different segments of the same descent group, who obtain land from a segment other than their own. Thus in the B group's case, if a member of the northern segment were to take land in Omazi section, he would only be a secondary right-holder (cf. Fig. 7). One E group man told me that he had asked a relative of his for permission to cultivate a particular piece of bush land. I was puzzled, since both were members of group E, and I had been told that this area was E group's land. Only later did I realize that the two men were from different segments of the same descent group, and so one of them had first to ask permission before he could cultivate. However people do not normally differentiate between primary and secondary right-holders in any but their own descent group. Thus if I had asked a non-E group man why the two men mentioned above were cultivating those particular fields, he would have replied that this was an E group area, and they were both members of the E descent group.

Secondary right-holders obtain land through asking permission of their fellow descent group members. But other kinsmen of segment members may be related through different descent groups; these fall into the category of tertiary right holders, which also includes non-kinsmen and people who obtain land through other means, such as affinity, friendship, or merely by asking permission; in short, it consists of anyone who is not a member of the descent group associated with the land, but obtains land through *jamaa* ties.

Secondary and tertiary right-holders can only obtain land with the consent of all members of the segment. Otherwise, as has been stated, a man with primary rights can come along, and in theory at least, turn a secondary or tertiary right-holder off the land. Normally, then, these people apply to the Elder of the segment for permission to cultivate the land. In the case of F group land they may submit a request through an Elder or apply directly to one of the Guardians. The latter have power to allocate any F group land, even, according to one Guardian, land outside their own segments. They themselves usually cultivate near to the spirit shrines.

If a man who is not a primary right-holder takes a field belonging to another descent group without permission, he can be turned off the land, or at least he could until very recently. The following case concerns a dispute between a man who under traditional rules had no right to the land he was cultivating and members of the segment which held the land.

CASE 6

Dispute over rights to a field

When the cultivation season opened in October 1965, M.A. wanted to cultivate an area of bush which belongs to the D group people. Without consulting any of the Elders of D group, he went and started to cut the bush.

The people who were primary right-holders of this field, led by the segment Elder, disputed his right to this field, and said that he was not a member of their descent group, much less of their segment. M.A. claimed that he had some right through his mother's mother. The D group members challenged him to bring forward any Elder who would substantiate his claim, but M.A. was unable to do this.

The dispute reached the ears of the Village Executive Officer, at the time a youth from southern Mafia (cf. Chapter 7), who went to look at the land, and pronounced it to be 'government land', since it had no coconut trees on it. He was thus saying that M.A. had a right to cultivate this land.

The D group people thereupon brought the matter before the VDC, which offered to divide the field in half, as a compromise measure. M.A. refused to accept this, and the disputants all but came to blows.

M.A. was now fairly sure of his ground, and went off to the court in Kilindoni where the judge (*hakimu*) told him to continue cultivating, as this was government land. Needless to say, M.A. did not tell the judge that he claimed this land through an ancestor, but that he, as a citizen, was cultivating government land.

The D group men despaired of their case, and finally gave up in disgust, and M.A. cultivated the field.

M.A. later contributed during the course of the agricultural cycle to the offerings made to the F group spirits. It may well be that, by so doing, not only was he ensuring the protection of his field, but also trying to act once again within the framework of village custom. The Guardians of group F accepted his contributions, and indeed, his active participation in the various rites, as if this actually were an F group field. This was M.A.'s intention. The field in question lay on the border between an F and a D group area, and thus it was easy for M.A. to begin claiming that in fact this was an F group field, and that since he himself is a member of F group, he was quite entitled to cultivate there.

He thus took three different lines of action at different stages of the dispute. In the first place, he maintained that he was a primary right-holder. When it became obvious that this was impossible to prove, he rejected the village customs, and said that this was 'government land'. In this he was supported by the Village Executive Officer, and rather half-heartedly by the VDC, and then by the judge in the Kilindoni court. In behaving this way, M.A. made himself very unpopular. He tried to redress matters by maintaining that the field in question was in fact an F group field, and he, as an F group man, had a perfect right to cultivate there. This he did by making offerings to the spirit, along with the neighbouring F group peoples. At the same time he ensured that the field was protected against the witchcraft of his enemies (cf. p. 68).

However, had M.A. asked to cultivate the land as a tertiary right-holder, it is unlikely that he would have been refused, for it is not uncommon to find tertiary and secondary right-holders outnumbering primary right-holders. This may be illustrated with reference to the B group genealogy (Fig. 7). The section in question, called Omazi, can be cultivated by all the people in segment (b) as these are the primary right-holders. However, only two of them actually did so in 1966, and the remaining four people in this section obtained their rights through affinal ties as follows:

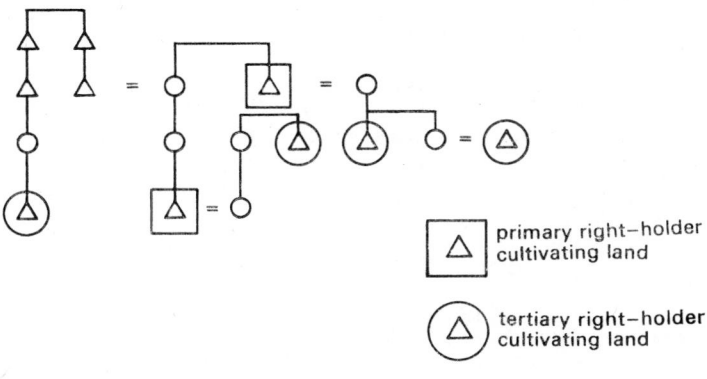

FIG. 9

People cultivating a B group section in 1966: obtaining land through affinal links

People may equally well use kinship links, as the following genealogy shows. This is an A group bush field, and the people marked in black are primary right-holders. They inherited A group membership through Makungu's first wife. The children of Makungu's second wife are not A group people, and they have used their kinship links through Makungu to obtain land, as tertiary holders.

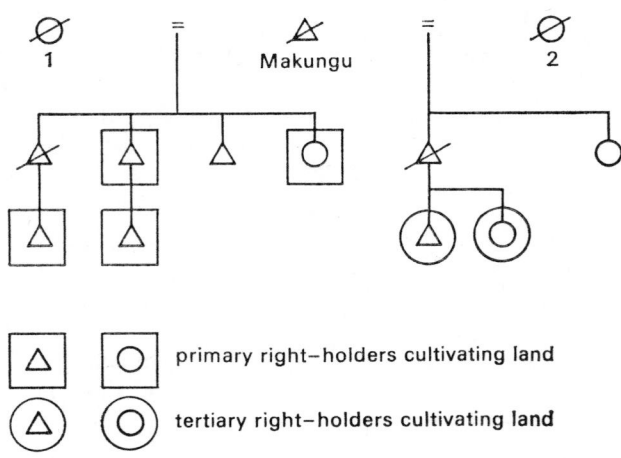

△   ○   primary right—holders cultivating land

Ⓐ   Ⓞ   tertiary right—holders cultivating land

FIG. 10

People cultivating an A group section in 1966: obtaining land through kinship links

Generally, it is not difficult for people without primary rights to obtain land, as the following case history shows.

CASE 7

Cultivation choices and tertiary rights

Masiku is aged about 32. He has cultivated land for 11 years. His FF, MF, and MM all hold descent group membership in a neighbouring village. His FM was an F group woman, and accordingly he has membership of this descent group through her.

His wife's ancestors were mainly from another northern village but through her FF she is a member of the C descent group. However, this group has no bush land. Thus in Minazini they can only obtain F group bush land.

Masiku cultivated F group land four times, and he cultivated meadow near to his coconut trees once. The remaining six years he has cultivated land which he obtained through other links. He says that he does not like to cultivate F group land, as it is far from the village, and he is a fisherman.

Thus most of the time Masiku did not cultivate land over which he had primary or even secondary rights.

Even those descent groups which hold little bush land admit outsiders, and a total of 20 per cent of the men cultivating bush land held by descent groups in 1966 were tertiary right-holders, who obtained land through their personal network as the following table shows:

TABLE 19
How rights to bush land were obtained in 1965–6

Name of d/g	Primary and secondary holders: through husband	through wife	Tertiary holders	Total cultivating bush land
A	6	0	1	7
B	3	1	3	7
D	5	1	2	8
E	7	1	0	8
F	47	11	15	73
	68 *	14†	21	103
	(67%)	(13%)	(20%)	(100%)

Notes: * In addition there were four single women who obtained rights through their own descent group membership.

† Because of the high rate of kin marriage many husbands and wives have at least one descent group in common. Thus in many cases, both husband and wife were primary or secondary right-holders, but usually they would say that they had obtained the land through the husband. Thus the above table does not reflect the number of wives who are in fact primary or secondary right-holders themselves.

Meadow land

Meadow fields are to be found in the village itself, and are part of the wards discussed in the last Chapter. The distribution of meadow land is shown on the map of the village (cf. Fig. 2). Some meadow areas are separated from each other by coconut trees and houses, although much of the meadow land in the south of the village, which is held by A, C, and D descent groups, stretches in a continuous belt, with each descent group holding a separate portion; the meadow land of groups E and F, on the other hand, is not divided up between them.[6]

The distribution of meadow land between the descent groups is exactly the reverse of that of bush land, for much of the meadow land in the village is held by A, B, C, and D groups, while the two descent groups which hold the largest amount of bush land—E and F—hold relatively little meadow land. Meadow land is cultivated in the main by three categories of people. First of all, old people and single women prefer meadow to bush land because the work is less demanding. Secondly, married women sometimes cultivate a small meadow field as a supplement to the main bush field. The third category is composed of those who find it inconvenient to be far away from the village. These include people who want to attend mosque daily, those who are politically very active, and fishermen. As is shown in Chapters 5 and 7, the majority of people active in religious affairs and politics are members of the A, B, and D descent groups, those very groups with the most meadow land.

It is not possible to give an estimate of the number of meadow fields available for each descent group in relation to the size of the group, as was done for the bush fields, because meadow fields vary so considerably in size. However, it is possible to say how many people cultivated with each descent group in 1966.

TABLE 20

Distribution of meadow land among descent groups in 1966

Descent group	No. of fields cultivated	% of total cultivated
No descent group	5	4
A	20	15
B	26	20
C	1	1
D	23	18
E and F	56	43
Total	131	100

As the table shows, more people cultivated with groups F and E than with the other descent groups. However, it should be remembered that these are two of the largest descent groups, and furthermore that all their land was cultivated, whereas much of the meadow land of the other descent groups, particularly A and D, lay fallow.

Allocation of meadow land

It is convenient to divide meadow land into three different types. The first is land attached to coconut trees. This land is usually considered to be a part of a coconut grove, and thus can be sold, inherited, etc. Even the government recognizes the permanent rights of an individual over such land, as the following case illustrates:

CASE 8

Dispute over rights to a meadow field

Athman owned coconut trees bordering a meadow field associated with the B descent group, of which he himself is a member. However, since he is also an F group member, he usually cultivated bush land, and allowed his classificatory grand-daughter to cultivate the meadow, along with her husband.

In 1965 the couple had a number of quarrels with accusations of infidelity on the part of the husband, and counter-accusations by the wife that her husband beat her unjustly. Finally both parties went to Kilindoni Court, and the husband, Hatibu, agreed to a divorce.

The following year, both parties were remarried. Athman's granddaughter was cultivating bush land with her new husband. Hatibu wished to continue to cultivate the meadow land with his new wife. They started to hoe the ground and sow seed.

Athman disputed their right to cultivate there, saying that this was his land, and he had not given them permission. Hatibu however replied that he was cultivating 'government land' and he had a perfect right to do so.

The matter was taken before the VDC, who were very puzzled about what to do in this case. Eventually they referred the matter to the judge of the court in Kilindoni. The judgement was that the land belonged to Athman, since the trees were his (he even had German documents giving him title to the trees). However Hatibu was to be allowed to cultivate the land until he had harvested his crop, since he had already begun to cultivate. This was agreed to by all the parties, although Athman was angry that Hatibu should remain even for a short time on his land.

The following year, Athman's own daughter went to cultivate this field. Hatibu protested, and said that this was his field, and he had cultivated there for a number of years. The matter again went before the VDC, but Hatibu, realizing that he had been defeated, failed to turn up at the hearing. The VDC members told Athman's daughter to continue cultivating the field.

This whole question of whether or not trees give a person rights to the adjacent land is a very difficult one. The case does not often arise in Minazini,[7] and in fact, it seems probable that the bad feelings caused by the divorce were a major factor in the dispute. Most villagers in Minazini recognize that meadow land, if it is bordered by coconut trees, is the property of the person who owns the trees.

The second type of meadow land is that which does not have trees attached to it, but which is nevertheless held by an individual or a small group by virtue of being cultivated on a permanent basis. This land is also inherited, and the heirs may hold it in common, with each taking it in turns to cultivate it, or if it is a large piece of land, they may divide it between them. It is very common for this type of land to be held by women, and for a woman to give it to her daughter before her death. Since there are no trees on it, the government would not recognize permanent rights to such land.

As I have already mentioned, women use meadow land as a security against divorce or widowhood, and they will seek to retain their rights in a piece of land by continuing to cultivate it even when they are married into another village.

The third type of meadow land is not cultivated on a permanent basis, nor are rights to it held by an individual or a sibling group. Rights to this type of land are more like rights to bush land; members of a descent group, or a segment, are primary holders. People who cultivate this type of land normally do so only for a year or so at a time, and their rights lapse after they have left it for more than a year.

The three types of meadow land are convertible. If a person cultivating the third category stays there for a long time, builds a fence, and uses fertilizer (cow dung) on the field, he or she establishes permanent individual rights over it, and the field may be inherited by the heirs; in other words, it becomes land of the second category. Similarly, if a person with category two land plants a few trees upon it, he or she establishes a completely inalienable right. The opposite may also apply. In some cases, people have sold their trees, but stipulated that they should retain the meadow land adjacent to it. Similarly, if a person with category two land abandons it, it will become land of category three. This is unlikely to happen, however, as it would probably be taken over by one of his or her relatives.

Meadow land, then, is obtained through ownership of coconut trees; through inheriting, being given, or creating permanent rights over a piece of land; through being a member of a descent group; or through asking permission.

Table 21 shows how meadow land rights were obtained in 1965–6:

TABLE 21
How meadow fields were obtained, 1965–6

Name of descent group	Ownership of trees	Permanent field	Descent Group membership	Asking permission	Total
no d/g	5	0	0	0	5
F and E	33	8	4	11	56
D	7	7	1	8	23
A and C	10	6	1	4	21
B	12	5	2	7	26
Total	67 (51%)	26 (20%)	8 (6%)	30 (23%)	131 (100%)

The table demonstrates the paramount importance of individual rights in the holding of meadow land. Fifty-one per cent of people cultivated land where they own coconut trees on or adjacent to their field, and a further 20 per cent cultivated land which they hold permanently. Only 6 per cent of people cultivating meadow land that year (1965–6) obtained it through descent group membership alone, although there is in fact a great deal more land of category three which lies fallow. However, as with bush fields, a sizeable minority (23 per cent) obtained land by asking permission. It is very noticeable that the majority of these people are close kinsmen (*jamaa sana*) of the primary holder, rather than distant kin, neighbours or friends; it is in fact much less easy to get permission to use someone else's meadow land, than to get bush land. The main reason for this is that people are afraid that outsiders will try to establish permanent rights, as Makungu did in Case 8.

It may be helpful at this point to summarize the differences between meadow and bush land, in order to see what factors lead people to cultivate one type of land rather than the other. Only a tiny minority, it should be remembered, cultivate both types in any one year, as a bush field requires the cultivator to live on it during the ripening of the crop, in order to protect it against pigs, birds, and monkeys. Those few couples who manage to cultivate a field of each kind generally have a main bush field, and a small area of meadow land; the latter will probably be next to that of a kinsman, who agrees to watch over it for them.

The first and perhaps the most important difference between the two types of land is that on bush land a person has a right to *some* land, as much as can be cultivated. With meadow land, on the other hand, except for category three land, held by a descent group, a man or woman has the right to a *particular* piece of land.

The second difference between meadow and bush land is that they are cultivated by different categories of people. On the whole young and middle-aged couples cultivate bush land. The reason for this is that they are better able to cope with the hard work involved (cutting bush, building fences, etc.) than older people. Bush land also tends to be cultivated by poorer households, because the crops ripen earlier, thus obviating sooner the necessity to buy staples for cash. Meadow land, on the other hand, is cultivated not only by elderly people and single women, but also by people who are involved in Islamic religious activities, and village politics, and who prefer to remain in the village all the year round, rather than spend five months out in the fields, as do those cultivating bush land.

Of course, descent group membership to some extent influences the choice between bush and meadow land. Members of descent group F tend to cultivate bush land more often than members of other descent groups, largely because most of the land of this group is bush. Another factor is that few members of this group are involved in political or religious activity, and thus it does not matter to them that they are away from the village. However, all in all, approximately the same number of bush and meadow fields are cultivated each year.

Methods of allocation of bush and meadow land differ too. As rights to meadow land are nearly all obtained through ownership of coconut trees or permanent rights over a piece of land, Elders play no part in allocating the land, although like any primary holders they may allow someone to use their land. Likewise, because no spirits or spirit shrines are associated with meadow land, there are no Guardians, nor are any rituals carried out in meadow fields during the agricultural season.

Another important difference is that the government recognizes permanent rights to meadow land, or at least those rights which can be validated by ownership of coconut trees. No such recognition is given to bush land, as Cases 4 and 6 demonstrate.

Rights to both types of land are essentially concerned with descent group membership. Most people obtain their coconut trees in the wards of their descent groups, hence the majority also hold their meadow fields in the same place. However, since meadow land bordered by coconut trees can be sold, and in a minority of cases, is sold to non-descent group members, it is possible for a primary right-holder on meadow land not to be a member of the descent group associated with that land. This situation could not occur with bush land; a primary right-holder must be a member of the descent group holding the land.

Descent, residence, and cultivation patterns

The purpose of this section is to show how people make choices about cultivation over a period of time, and to see whether people always cultivate with the same descent group each year, or whether they utilize all the descent groups in which they can claim membership, in order to obtain land rights. It will then be possible to see to what extent residence influences cultivation choices.

All households have a certain amount of choice about where they cultivate. They can choose between cultivating with the husband's or wife's descent group(s), and between cultivating descent group or non-descent group land. However not all people belong to more than one descent group, so their choice is limited in this respect, although they can always utilize the *jamaa* in order to obtain land from other groups.

In the following table a sample of fifty men is examined for the way in which they made their cultivation choices over a period of six years, from 1961–7.

TABLE 22
Descent groups and cultivation choices, 1961–7

Number of descent groups of which a member:							Nos. of descent group members
0 d/g	1 d/g	2 d/g	3 d/g	4 d/g	5 d/g	Total	cultivating with
3	4	1	—	—	—	8	0 d/g
—	15	8	3	1	—	27	1 d/g
—	—	7	3	2	1	13	2 d/g
—	—	—	1	—	1	2	3 d/g
—	—	—	—	—	—	—	4 d/g
—	—	—	—	—	—	—	5 d/g
3	19	16	7	3	2	50	Totals

The above table shows that 28 men (56 per cent of the sample) had membership of more than one descent group. A majority of these (15) had actually used their membership of more than one descent group in order to obtain land rights during that period. This is important because it reinforces the point that descent group membership is not 'closed' in regard to cultivation choices. Membership is determined by birth, and if a man is a member of more than one group, he can, and does, utilize his rights in several groups in order to obtain land.

The conclusions to be drawn from the table are borne out by the following case history. It concerns a man in his early thirties, who can remember where he has cultivated every year since he was old enough to have his own field.

CASE 9

Ahmed's cultivation choices

Descent group membership —group F (through FF)
group B (through FM, MM—his MF was an immigrant from the mainland)
Wife's descent groups —group F only
Period of cultivation —1952–67
Patterns of cultivation choices—group F—10 times
group B—4 times
tertiary holder—once

Ahmed resides in the F group ward. He has cultivated F group land more frequently than any other. This however is to be expected in view of the fact that it is much more plentiful than B group land. Even so he has cultivated B group land four times out of a possible fifteen. And he has utilized the two descent group options open to him; in other words he has taken up rights in both the descent groups in which he claims membership.

Ahmed claims to prefer F group land, because he says that it is always protected by a spirit, and there is no danger of fields being bewitched. (This is in contrast to Masiku in Case 7, who said that he preferred *not* to use group F land, because it was far from the village, and he was a fisherman.) However it may be that for some reason Ahmed failed to get the F group land he wanted, and so had to go elsewhere. This happened in the 1966–7 season, when the land allocated to him through his father-in-law was taken by another man (cf. Case 4).

To what extent does choice of residence affect cultivation choices? Let us examine again our sample of fifty men. For a man who is a member of more than one descent group, and who is living on ward land held by one of those groups, the following possibilities are available: (1) to cultivate *only* with the descent group with which he is residing, (2) to cultivate with this descent group *and* with others of which he or his wife are members, (3) to cultivate with other descent group(s) with which they are not residing, but of which they are still members, or finally (4) to obtain land through their *jamaa*.

Of our sample of 50 men, only 28 are members of more than one descent group. Between 1961 and 1967, only 8 of the 28 men cultivated solely with the descent group with which they reside, thus ignoring their potential choices. However, 14 other men cultivated both with their descent group of residence and with other groups of which they are members. The remainder did not cultivate with the group with which they were residing, but with other groups to which they belong; the sole exception was one man who ignored his rights through all his descent groups and preferred to cultivate land which he obtained through his *jamaa*.

The conclusion to be drawn from this is that choice of residence does not necessarily affect choice of cultivation. Half of the men who had a choice cultivated not only with the descent group with which they were residing, but also with other groups of which they were members. In other words, having made a choice in regard to residence, a person is not thereby confined in his choice with regard to cultivation.

Fourteen of the remainder of the sample are members of one group only, and the majority of them (11) cultivated exclusively with that group; the remainder obtained their land through their *jamaa* links. Three other men in the sample had no descent group membership at all, but were living on ward land; they tended to obtain their land from the descent group of the ward in which they resided. Finally, the remaining category of five men includes some living on non-ward land, and some living in wards where they do not have rights through descent group membership. However, all these people are members of at least one descent group in the village, and they used their descent group links in order to obtain land. In other words, the fact that a man might not be residing with one of his descent groups does not mean that he cannot obtain land rights through descent. Nor does it mean that, if a man resides with a descent group of which he is not a member, he would also obtain land through the same group; normally he obtains land through his own groups. Only those men who are not members of any descent group tend to reside *and* cultivate with the same descent group; usually they obtain permission through affinal links.

Finally we might look at the question of cultivation choices from the point of view of each descent group and ask what proportion of members took up their rights to land. The following table gives the choices of all the male members of each descent group over a period of six years.

TABLE 23

Proportion of descent group members cultivating descent group land, 1960–6

Name of descent group	Proportion of male members using land at least once
A	70%
B	58%
C	18%
D	70%
E	70%
F	82%

It will be remembered that groups E and F own the largest amount of bush land (cf. Table 17). Conversely groups A and D hold the largest amount of meadow land. It is thus to be expected that the majority of their members would cultivate with these groups fairly often, even if not every year. Group B members appear to use their land less often, and one of the reasons is that there is less available.

Group C, as has already been remarked, possesses no bush land, and only a little meadow land, so that it is not surprising that most of its members look to other descent groups in order to obtain land.

However it is interesting to compare this table (23) with Table 16 at the end of the last chapter, and to note that the three descent groups with which a majority of members affiliate for residence purposes are also the three groups in which the highest proportion of members affiliate for cultivation purposes. Similarly, those groups with only a minority of members residing in their wards have fewer members cultivating their land. However the fact that the D descent group has a minority of members residing in its ward, while a large proportion cultivate its land, suggests that there is not always a direct correlation. People who are not residing on group D's land nevertheless cultivate there; this emphasizes my earlier point that residence choices do not determine cultivation choices.

Conclusion

Cultivable land is seen by Minazini people as the property of descent groups, descent group segments, and, in the case of some meadow land, of individuals. People can obtain rights as primary holders through membership of descent group segments, or alternatively they can obtain secondary and tertiary rights using other ties, that is, through their *jamaa*. In fact most people, over a period of time, use different links to obtain land, including, but rarely exclusively, that of the descent group with which they are residing. Choices are not always as wide in practice as in theory, even for people who are members of more than one descent group, because there may be localized shortages within a particular segment, or people may be precluded from utilizing their potential choices because of physical or economic constraints like old age, the breakdown of a marriage, or the need to obtain an early harvest.

On the whole, however, as I have shown in the preceding section, the gap between ideology—that people can utilize descent group and *jamaa* ties to obtain land—and practice is not wide, for over a period of time there are few people who neglect any of their potential choices. Those who are members of more than one group will almost always take up all of their rights to cultivable land at some time or other. Furthermore such people are not necessarily attracted more frequently to the land of the descent group with which they are residing —residence is in no way a 'closing' factor in the situation.

Choices are wide not only because people may belong to more than one group, and can also utilize their *jamaa* links, but also because on the whole, as I have shown, land is not yet a very scarce resource. In the second part of the book, we shall be concerned with resources—socio-religious status and political power—which *are* scarce. In seeking access to these, people are not able to move around from one descent group to another as they can to obtain land. Those who would wield power must, as I shall demonstrate, commit themselves to a single group.

CHAPTER 5

THE SOCIO-RELIGIOUS HIERARCHY:
(1) ISLAM

In the preceding chapters, Minazini society has been viewed in terms of two frameworks—the descent groups and the *jamaa*, with emphasis on the former. In the second part of this book, I propose to examine the relationship between the descent groups and a socio-religious hierarchy generated by a perceived antithesis between orthodox Islamic observance and spirit possession; this hierarchy is significant not only in the religious but also in the political sphere. In these contexts, the descent groups are not all of the same order, as they are in regard to land-holding; some groups and their members have higher status, and hence greater access to power than others. In order to understand why this is so, it is necessary first of all to recall the distinction made in the first chapter between 'tribes'.

Population categories

Minazini people see themselves not only as members of descent groups, but also as members of 'tribes' (in fact, these categories are not tribes in any accepted sense, as I have said in the first chapter, but they are referred to by the Swahili term *kabila*, generally translated as 'tribe'; hence I use this term for lack of any other). In Minazini, as in most of the northern villages, the majority of the villagers call themselves Pokomo and/or Mbwera. The former are supposed to have been more recent arrivals on the Island than the latter, and until two generations ago, to have lived separately. In Minazini, members of descent group F, together with a few immigrants from other northern villages, are classified as Pokomo. Members of the five remaining descent groups form the category of Mbwera. Since German times, when formerly separate hamlets amalgamated to form the village of

Minazini (cf. Chapter 2), Pokomo and Mbwera have been inter-marrying, so that today, just over one-third of the population belongs to both categories.

Other 'tribal' categories in the village are formed by the Gunya, and by the descendants of slaves, who claim to be members of such inland tribes as the Zaramo, Nyasa, and Yao.

The division between Pokomo and Mbwera assumes greatest importance in the context of orthodox Islamic activity, political affairs and spirit possession. The two former fields, which are mono-polized by the Mbwera and the Gunya, are discussed in this chapter and Chapter 7, while spirit possession, almost entirely the preserve of the Pokomo (i.e. descent group F members), is discussed in Chapter 6.

The socio-religious hierarchy

In order to understand the hierarchical nature of Minazini society, we have to grasp the relationship between three models—not only those of the cognatic descent groups and the tribal categories of Mbwera and Pokomo which have already been discussed, but also the East African coastal three-tier hierarchical system, composed broadly of Arabs, free born (*waungwana*) and descendants of slaves (*watumwa*). Variations on the same theme appear all over the coast (cf., Bujra 1968 on the northern Kenya coast, and Lienhardt 1968 for in-formation on the southern Tanzania coast). The categories are less clear-cut than formerly because of the growth of African nationalism and the desirability of aligning oneself, in public at any rate, with 'Africanness'. However, in Minazini, the basic values remain the same; Arabs, and everything with which they are associated (dress, way of speech, manners, orthodox Islamic practices) are 'good', and to be emulated. The very word for civilization in Swahili (*ustaarabu*) is derived from an Arabic word meaning 'Arabness'.

Minazini, like most coastal villages, has marked status differentia-tion, although not conforming exactly to the model given above. To begin with, there are only two adult Arabs in the village, a man and wife, and there are only twenty adult descendants of slaves, so that the vast majority would fall into the category of 'free born'. Even within this category, however, there are marked differences in status.

Status is of two types, which are distinguishable only in certain contexts—social status, determined by birth (which is always ascribed, and thus connected with descent group membership), and Islamic religious status (which may be achieved or ascribed). Unless otherwise stated, 'status' in this chapter will refer to socio-religious status.

Next to the Arabs, the people of highest status in Minazini are the Gunya Sharifs, and after them the rest of the Gunya. They claim to be 'almost' Arabs in descent, and this claim is accepted by the rest of the villagers, although Arabs themselves would be unlikely to accept such claims. Only two of the Gunya are Sharifs, the Village Chairman (cf. Chapter 7) and his sister. Sharifs are said to be the descendants of the Prophet, and as such to have the particular favour of God, and to be able to pass on blessing (*baraka*) to those who touch them. In some parts of the coast, Sharifs have their hands kissed in greeting, but this is not done in Minazini. Nonetheless the Sharifs are highly esteemed, and people go to pray at the Sharifs' ancestors' graves in preference to the graves of their own ancestors. Sharifs in Minazini enjoy high religious status by ascription, even though they do not participate actively in any of the orthodox Islamic activities.

Along with the Gunya immigrants from Zanzibar, which is thought to be a more 'civilized' place than Mafia, also enjoy high status. The Zanzibari immigrants in Minazini consist of the children of a Sheikh who settled in the village, and married an Mbwera woman. One of his sons is the Sheikh of Minazini.

Next to them in the hierarchy come the Mbwera, who consider themselves to be superior to the Pokomo for several reasons. First of all, they have been in the area for a longer time: they often refer to themselves as 'real Minazini people' in opposition to the Pokomo who are said to be more recent arrivals. Secondly, it is from the ranks of the Mbwera that the majority of pious and learned men in the village are drawn. Such people despise the Pokomo not only because they neglect orthodox Islamic activities, but also because the latter engage in spirit possession cults which are thought, in this area, to be antithetical to orthodox Islam (cf. Caplan 1974).

At this level it is possible to distinguish between social and religious status. Socially the Pokomo fall into the category of the 'free born' and are therefore superior to the ex-slaves. However, it is possible for an ex-slave, who is not involved in spirit possession cults, to become a Koranic teacher and thus be given a higher *religious* status than many Pokomo, particularly those highly involved in spirit possession cults, even though ex-slaves are of lower *social* status, since they are not among the 'free born'.

But despite such a partial dissociation of religious and social status, by and large there is a single hierarchy of socio-religious status recognized in Minazini. It may be summarized as follows:

TABLE 24
Socio-religious hierarchy

Arabs
Sharifs
other Gunya
Zanzibar immigrants
'pure' Mbwera
people of mixed Mbwera–Pokomo descent
'pure' Pokomo
ex-slaves

This hierarchy is important in the political sphere, for power has been traditionally wielded by religious leaders in the village, with a combination of high social status and piety as the essential prerequisites for office (compare Bujra 1973). This value system has until recently been accepted by everyone in the population; 'good' is equated with high socio-religious status, and 'bad' with low status, and particularly with spirit possession.

However these distinctions are not absolute, because there are still many people of mixed descent, who can use their membership of different groups in different contexts, and this must be borne in mind throughout this latter part of the book. Such a system of overlapping categories is able to co-exist with a system of stratification because, in theory, although rarely in practice, a distinction can be made between the two spheres.

Another important point which must be kept in mind when discussing the social hierarchy is that, on the whole, wealth cuts right across it. That is to say, there are people of high status who are not particularly wealthy, while some people of low status are among the wealthiest in the village.

It is difficult to measure incomes, as I have already said, but a useful index of wealth is the number of coconut trees owned, since any surplus cash income is usually invested in coconut trees. There are twenty men in the village who own 200 trees or more, and they belong to the following categories in the population: one is the Arab man, two are the children of Zanzibari immigrants, eight are 'pure' Mbwera, five of mixed Mbwera–Pokomo descent and five are 'pure' Pokomo. In short, then, apart from the Arab and Zanzibaris no single category can claim a disproportionate number of rich men.

To a certain extent, wealth *can* be translated into higher status, for wealthier people can use their income to buy staples, and thus need to spend less time growing crops. The leisure thus acquired can be spent in pursuing religious learning, and attending mosque assiduously. Wealthier people can also ensure that their children have a good education in a Koran school.

On the other hand, wealth cannot be used to acquire power over other people. Wealthier people in the village do not act as money-lenders, nor do they hire poorer people to work on their land, as is the case elsewhere. So in this sense, wealth is not an important variable when discussing the workings of the social hierarchy.

Before returning in Chapter 7 to discuss again the relationship between the descent groups and the social hierarchy, and the implication of this in the political field, I shall first discuss the way in which the hierarchy is generated, that is through orthodox Islamic activities, and their antithesis, spirit possession activities, the subject of the next chapter.

Islamic activities

Islam is the universal religion in the village. With the sole exception of the Arab, who is an Ibadhi, the population adheres to the Shafei school of the Sunnis. This means that certain ritual practices are carried out by everyone in the village. These I have termed 'universal rituals': they include rites of passage and certain communal rituals. A second category is formed by what I term 'general' rituals; unlike the universal rituals, they are not compulsory, but they are carried out by a large number of people. The most important rituals in this category are those of the *tarika*, or mystical orders. Finally, there is a third category which I term 'special rituals', which are only carried out by the very pious; the most important is regular attendance at Friday mosque.

Universal Islamic practices

Two types of ritual may be categorized as 'universal' in Minazini. They are the life crisis rituals—at birth, puberty, marriage, and death, and the annual communal rituals involving the whole village—the fast of Ramadhan, the *Maulid*[1] (celebration of the Prophet's birthday), and the circumambulation and blessing of the village (*kuzingua mji*).

RITES OF PASSAGE

The rituals surrounding birth, marriage, and death are carried out according to Islamic law, although, particularly in the case of marriage, there are many embellishments. The presence of a *mwalim* to lead the prayers and conduct the ritual is necessary on all of these occasions. In the case of marriages and funerals, which are the two most important life crisis rituals, the Sheikh is always called upon. In this context, he is 'our Sheikh', i.e. the Sheikh of the whole village, and not just the A group's Sheikh. In 1966, the government declared that a *Kadhi* (religious judge) should be appointed in each village, and the VDC members chose the Sheikh, so that his position is now official, and no one else may officiate over marriages in the village.

Although the whole population carries out the same type of ritual for births, marriages, and deaths, the same is not true of puberty rituals, that is, circumcision for boys, and ear-piercing, and later, ritual washing at first menstruation for girls (cf. Caplan *in the press*). It is noticeable that the most pious members of the village have been the first to take advantage of the facilities offered for circumcising boys in Kilindoni hospital, and they then return to the village to hold a 'coming-out' feast, usually with a Koranic reading (*hitima*) or else a *Maulid* reading. Other people in the village have their sons circumcised by a local 'expert', who also conducts a long and complicated ceremony, consisting of dancing and singing, most of the symbolism of which is sexual in content.

The same applies to rites held for girls. Ear-piercing, while it is considered essential, is a minor rite, and is always held on the day when a feast is given for newly circumcised boys. However when a girl menstruates for the first time, she has to be ritually washed by her sexual instructress (*mkunga*), and taught how to wear her menstrual cloth, and to wash carefully. She is then formally secluded inside her parents' house until her marriage has been arranged. The daughters of people of high socio-religious status are merely washed, and usually a few prayers recited by the woman present. However, in families of low socio-religious status, a ceremony called *unyago* is arranged—this involves calling in a female 'expert' who, by song, dance, and mime, teaches the girl what will be expected of her in her role as wife.

In short then, it is usually people of high socio-religious status who practise the more 'Islamic' form of puberty ceremonies, while other people generally prefer to hold the long and complicated rites involving sexual instruction.

COMMUNAL RITUALS

The three communal rituals, held annually, involve the whole village, and emphasize that it is a ritual unit. While the main impetus tends to come from people of high socio-religious status, people of all categories in the village—ex-slaves, Gunya, Mbwera, and Pokomo—participate in the arrangements, and attend the feasts connected with the rituals. Contributions to the feasts at the *Maulid* and the blessing of the village are made through descent groups, although cooking for the feasts is not carried out by the descent groups, as is the case with life crisis rituals, but by the whole village as a unit. Although these annual rituals are usually carried out by all categories in the village, as I have said, the 'religious' aspect is generally dominated by people of high socio-religious status. Thus for instance although everyone fasts during Ramadhan, it is mainly high status people who attend mosque each evening, and who also fast the extra seven days at the end of the month of Ramadhan. Similarly, it is such people who lead the *Maulid* reading, which lasts all night, before the feast is held; they also lead the procession of men who spend three days circumambulating the village, reading the Koran, to 'cast out evil', before the cow, to the purchase of which all have contributed, is slaughtered and the meat cooked.[2]

General Islamic practices

Three types of practices fall into this category—kinship rituals to remember the ancestors, and ask forgiveness for sins; the Koranic education of children; and the rituals of the *tarika* societies.

KINSHIP RITUALS

Koranic readings to remember the ancestors (*hitima ya kuarehemu wazee*) are usually held on ancestral graves, and involve a reading of the whole Koran (*hitima*), and the naming of all the ancestors who can be remembered by those present. Readings may be held in connection with a life crisis ritual, but they are also held during the Islamic seventh month, when the graves are cleared. In addition, some people institute a special type of *hitima*, known as *Mwanasha*, on the anniversary of a parent's death; people of all categories hold *hitima* of this type, and the wealthier ones also hold a small feast.

KORAN SCHOOLS

The second item of general Islamic observance is that of the education of children in Koran schools. There are four such schools in Minazini, with a total of 67 children, which is rather less than half of the children of an age to attend (i.e. over six or seven years). They are taught to read the Koran in Arabic, although they do not understand what they read, and they learn to write Swahili in Arabic script.

Two of the teachers (*walim*) who hold Koran classes are members of descent group A (and of no other group in Minazini), and reside in the A group's wards—one, who is the brother of the Sheikh, lives in the A ward proper, and one in the breakaway Crossroads ward. Most of the children living in the A ward, together with the Gunya children, are taught by these men. A third teacher is a member of descent groups D and E, who is renowned for his piety and learning; his pupils come from wards D and E. The fourth teacher is a member of descent group F, and he is the only *mwalim* in the village who publicly condones spirit possession, and helps occasionally in certain of those rituals considered less reprehensible (cf. Chapter 6).

Most of the children sent to a Koran school are those of parents who were themselves educated in this way; a higher proportion of the children of high status are educated in Koran schools than are the children of people of low status. Even so, there is a sizeable minority of children, whose parents are highly involved in spirit possession cults, who do go to Koran schools. This is the kind of situation which exemplifies my earlier point about the difficulties of making absolute distinctions in this society. After all, Islam *is* the universal religion in Minazini and the ability to read the Koran confers considerable prestige. Furthermore a Koranic education was, until very recently, the sole means of acquiring literacy. However if a comparison is made between members of descent group F and members of descent group A considerable differences in literacy rates would be found. In the latter group most male and many female members are able to read the Koran, and write Swahili in Arabic script, while very few members of the former group are able to do so.

Nowadays there is a government school between Minazini and a neighbouring village, and all the children are supposed to attend. However there has been considerable apathy and indeed opposition to a secular education (identified in the villagers' minds with a 'mission' or Christian education), and particularly about sending girls to school, and keeping them there until they have completed their courses, instead of secluding them at puberty in preparation for marriage. It is significant that most of this opposition has come not from the most pious parents of high status, but from parents of lower social status. The former have been the first to send their children, even girls, to government schools, while still of course insisting that the children read the Koran in the evenings and at weekends. The reason for this is that not only do such people claim to respect knowledge (*elimu*), but they have been quick to perceive the benefits of such an education. One of the most important of these is winning the approval of government officials by conforming to 'progressive' ideals, and, as will be seen in Chapter 7, this is important in maintaining their political position. Parents of low status, on the other hand, usually lack the sophistication to see any benefits deriving from a secular education, although they rationalize their opposition by claiming that secular schooling prevents the children from getting a proper Koranic education.

SUFI MYSTICAL ORDERS (*TARIKA*)

The most important rituals in this general category are those of the *tarika* societies. In Arabic, *tariq* means 'way, road, or path' but it has come to have a mystical connotation, meaning 'the whole system of rites for spiritual training laid down for communal life in the various Muslim orders' (Gibb and Kramers, 1961:573). In Minazini people are devotees of the Qadiriyya *tarika*, which was started by Seyyid Abd al-Qadir of Baghdad, and introduced into East Africa via Somalia and Zanzibar (cf. Trimingham 1964). The most important *tarika* ritual, indeed the only one generally performed by the devotees in Mafia, is the celebration of the founder's anniversary (*ziara*), which may be held on an Islamic feast-day.

Tarika rituals are characterized by the use of *dhikiri*, which Trimingham has defined as 'the remembrance of God by the repetition of His name and attributes; co-ordinated, when recited in congregation, with breathing techniques and physical movements' (ibid:96). It is thought that spiritual effects can be achieved through the rhythmical swaying and jumping, together with constant repetition of 'Allah, Allah'. One woman claimed that, after practising *dhikiri* for a long time, if she closed her eyes she could see the Prophet Mohammed. In addition to the congregational recitation of the *dhikiri*, there is singing in both Swahili and Arabic, led by the officials of the *tarika*.

Branches of the *tarika* are generally to be found in all the villages of Mafia. Each society has allegiance to a Sheikh, and sometimes there is considerable rivalry between the Sheikhs and their societies. The organization of all *tarika* societies, however, is basically the same. There are four types of officials—the Sheikh's deputies, known as *halifa*, who are the most important, the *shawishi*, who carry the banners, and are in charge of cooking, the *rishidi*, who help with leading the chanting, and finally, the *aba*, who call all the people together and are responsible for procuring the cow killed for the feast. There are usually at least two officials, a man and a woman, of each type in each village branch. The Sheikh appoints officials in each village branch of the society; they are chosen either directly by him or else on the advice of other officials in that branch, if he is not familiar with the village. Most men and women succeed near relatives, usually a parent, and indeed, in Minazini, the *tarika* societies are dominated by a number of close kinsmen belonging to descent groups A and E respectively.

Rituals involve a great deal of organization, as followers of the same Sheikh come together from a number of villages and have to be fed on arrival in early evening, and again the following morning. Frequently *ziara* attract around five hundred people. Money and rice are provided by the members of the host branch, and they also pay the Sheikh's travelling expenses if he is coming from another village. The largest contributions are made by the society officials, who give between 10s. and 20s., while ordinary members give 2s. each.

Preparations take at least a week, although plans are laid long before this. Women married outside the village return to help in the preparations (women retain the membership of the branch they joined as girls, and do not change on marriage). The specially appointed site of the *ziara* (known as *zawiya*) has to be cleared of the weeds which have sprung up since the previous year, and any fences and shelters which have become broken down are repaired. In addition the cooking preparations involve an army of helpers, and most of the officials, as well as ordinary members of the host society, are kept busy for the whole week preceding the *ziara*.

Undoubtedly one of the reasons for the large attendance at the *ziara*, apart from the genuine religious fervour generated, is the opportunity to meet old friends and dispersed relatives, as well as to wear new clothes, and be admired by members of the opposite sex. In spite of the segregation of men and women in the ritual, it is easy to slip away to a rendezvous in the darkness. One young man remarked cynically 'A *ziara* is something of a picnic' (using the English word).

In Minazini there are two *tarika* societies, one of which is led by the A group Sheikh, and the other by a Sheikh who lives in a southern village. The latter only visits Minazini once a year on the occasion of his *ziara*. Almost everyone in Minazini is a member of one of the two societies. People are usually recruited when they are quite young, and taken along by a relative to the Sheikh, who gives them sweetened water (*ijazi*) and recites prayers with them, after they have stated their wish to become a member of the society and a follower of the Sheikh.

The larger of the two Minazini societies is that which is centred on the E group's ward, and which is dominated by members of E and F descent groups; these are the followers of the southern Sheikh. The smaller society is led by the Minazini Sheikh, and the *zawiya* (site) is in the main ward of group A, in the south of the village. The Sheikh of this latter society, like his father before him, refuses to accept as followers those who are involved in land spirit possession (cf. next chapter). This effectively excludes most of the people who are members of descent group F.

CASE 10

The dispute of the Sheikhs

The *tarika* were only introduced into Minazini about forty years ago, by Sheikhs coming from Zanzibar. Three of these Sheikhs settled in three northern Mafian villages, the first of which was Minazini. The second and third Sheikhs were linked by the fact that they had been the pupils of the same Sheikh in Zanzibar. Each Sheikh formed a society, and they gathered followers about themselves, drawn not only from the villages in which they were living, but also from other villages.

A new mosque was built in another northern village, and the three Sheikhs were invited to the consecration. However, the third Sheikh was late in arriving, and the other two had decided to start without him. When he finally arrived, he was very angry, and severed relations with the other two Sheikhs. After this, each *tarika* society held its rituals without inviting members of the other societies. Later however the second and third Sheikhs made up their quarrel, but the first and third Sheikhs remained estranged. The quarrel was further exacerbated by a dispute over a woman whom both Sheikhs wished to marry.

After some time, the third Sheikh moved to southern Mafia, and his successor still lives there today. The second Sheikh died without a successor, and his society merged with that of the third Sheikh. But the rift between the first (Minazini) Sheikh and the southern Sheikh persists until this day. On the whole, each Sheikh draws his supporters from different villages, but in a few villages, there are followers of both Sheikhs.

Because the Sheikhs had quarrelled, people had to take sides, and support the Sheikh who led the society of which they were members. At one time, it seems that affiliation to a particular Sheikh was not associated with descent group membership, as it is today. The Imam of the Minazini mosque, a member of descent groups A, B, and D, who lives in the main A ward, was formerly a member of the southern Sheikh's society, and he held the highest post—that of *halifa*, or Sheikh's deputy. However the Minazini Sheikh had married his classificatory sister, and after the dispute between the Sheikhs, he allowed himself to be persuaded to attend the *ziara* of the Minazini Sheikh. Senior members of his own society discovered this, and arraigned him in public, forcing him to leave their society. He then joined forces with his brother-in-law, the Minazini Sheikh, and later the son of the latter (who is now the Minazini Sheikh) married his daughter. The process of the dispute is shown in the diagram below:

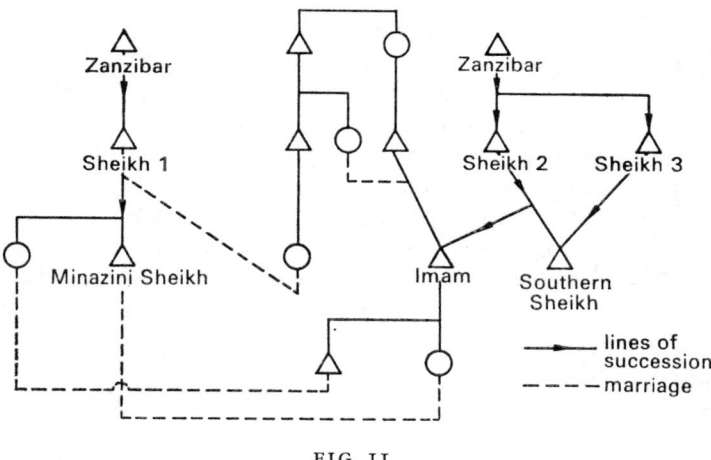

FIG. II

The dispute between the Sheikhs, and the Imam's change in affiliation

The Imam became *halifa* of the Minazini Sheikh's *tarika* society, and subsequently Imam of the Friday mosque. As will be shown, the Imam and the Sheikh and their kin dominate the political as well as the religious life of the village. It may in fact have been the case that the Imam thought he would have more to gain by joining the society of the Minazini Sheikh, who was not only his kinsman and affine, but also neighbour and fellow descent group member, than by continuing to ally himself with a Sheikh so removed from village affairs as the southern Sheikh.

Whatever may have been the position a generation ago, the fact now is that the cleavage between the two societies reflects other cleavages in Minazini society. The majority of people in the Minazini Sheikh's society are members of descent group A, together with pious people from the other Mbwera descent groups, who reject spirit possession in its 'worst' forms. And the officials of this society also dominate the Friday mosque, as well as the formal political institutions in the village (cf. Chapter 7).

As already mentioned, the headquarters of the two Minazini groups are in the wards of groups A and E. It is likely that there was a correlation between the segmentation of group E from group A, to which I have previously referred in Chapter 2, and the affiliation of the members of the descent groups to different *tarika* societies. It is possible that the members of group E joined the southern Sheikh's *tarika* society as a method of demonstrating their independence of the parent group A. Alternatively, it is possible that the original break between groups A and E was caused by the division of the village into followers of the Minazini and southern Sheikhs.

A similar process is shown by the present affiliations of the members of descent group B. The segment which has remained in the northern ward (cf. Chapter 2) has affiliated itself to the southern Sheikh, and its members participate in the *ziara* held in group E's ward. That segment which now resides in the south of the village, on the other hand, is affiliated with the *tarika* society of the Minazini Sheikh; this is one aspect of the attempts of the members of this segment to raise their social status, which they have also tried to do by attending mosque regularly and practising more discriminatory marriage policies.

Affiliation to the two societies in Minazini, in the case of the A, E, and F groups is now decided almost exclusively along descent group lines, while the members of the remaining groups are more evenly distributed between the two societies as Table 25 indicates.

Tarika society affiliation is thus connected with both the social hierarchy and the descent groups. The Minazini Sheikh's society is small and exclusive; it includes most people of high status, and specifically excludes people who practise spirit possession, i.e. people of low status. It includes most people who are members of descent group A, and excludes most of the members of groups E and F.

But again, the distinction is not absolute because the descent groups are so heavily inter-married, that the cleavage between the two societies has not resulted in a complete split in the village. Husbands and wives may belong to different societies, just as they may belong to different descent groups, and their children will choose membership of the one society or the other.

TABLE 25
Descent group membership and affiliation to tarika societies

Descent group	Minazini Sheikh's tarika society	Southern Sheikh's tarika society
A	80%	20%
B	48%	52%
C	53%	47%
D	30%	70%
E	5%	95%
F	14%	86%
Total male[3] pop.	38%	62%

Special Islamic practices

This category of Islamic observances is carried out only by the most pious people in the village, who are generally also those of the highest social status. It includes mosque attendance on Fridays and holy days, daily prayers, and the pursuit of higher Koranic learning.

There are four mosques in Minazini, one each in the wards of descent groups D and F, one in the main A group ward, and a fourth, built just before this study was carried out, in the ward of the break-away segment of group A, residing in the Crossroads area of the village. The opening of this mosque emphasizes still further the split between the main descent group, with its ward in the south of the village, and the breakaway segment. The mosques located in the F group's ward and also the two in the A group's wards are used daily for prayers at the set hours, both by the people living in the ward and by anyone passing by who wishes to use them; thus members of descent group A would pray in the mosque of the F group's ward, if they happened to be in the area.

The Friday mosque lies in the D group's ward, half-way between the wards of groups A and F (cf. map of village). This mosque is attended by about 24 per cent of the adult male population on a regular basis, i.e. on Fridays and holy days. However there is a considerable difference in the numbers attending from the various descent groups, as the following table shows:

TABLE 26
Friday mosque attendance and descent group membership

Name of descent group	Male members attending mosque No.	
A	16	50%
B	9	16%
C	7	25%
D	13	26%
E	7	16%
F	11	10%
Total	63	24%

Most of the official posts attached to the mosque are held by members of group A. The Imam, the two deputy Imams, and one of the two *muedhin* (who make the call to prayer), are all members of this descent group (cf. Fig. 14, Chapter 7). Most of these mosque officials also hold high posts in the *tarika* society of the Minazini Sheikh. The Imam himself has already been discussed in Case 10 earlier in this chapter. His son and a classificatory son are the deputy Imams. The two *muedhin* are both Koranic teachers; one is a member of group D and the other the leader of the breakaway segment (whose ward is in the Crossroads area) from group A. The former man is the only non-A group member who is an office holder in the Friday mosque, and he is also the only man who is neither a member of the Minazini Sheikh's *tarika* society nor closely related to the Sheikh either by descent or affinity.

At the time I began my field-work in 1965 women were not allowed to attend mosque, in spite of the fact that some of them were known to be pious and learned, and to pray daily; some also held important posts in the *tarika* societies. However the following year some of the women in a neighbouring village began to attend the Friday mosque there, after the visit of a crusading Sheikh from the mainland, who professed himself horrified to find women excluded. The Minazini women soon followed suit in their own village and the wives and daughters of men of high religious status, mostly members of descent group A, were the first to attend.

Descent group A, then, in spite of its small size (cf. Table 5) dominates most positions of importance in the context of orthodox Islam (cf. Fig. 14, Chapter 7). What of the other men of high socio-religious status? The Arab is an Ibadhi Muslim, and does not attend mosque, or participate in any of the other Islamic rituals, with the sole exception of the village *Maulid*. Gunya men likewise, in spite of the fact that all of them have had a Koranic education, and one has the status of a *mwalim*, take very little part in orthodox religious activities; only one of their number attends mosque, and that very irregularly, and none is a member of a *tarika* society. This fits in with their 'stranger' status, which they sometimes invoke for political ends, as will be shown in Chapter 7. Gunya women, on the other hand, do participate in the *tarika*, and one is an official (*mrishidi*) of the Minazini Sheikh's *tarika* society.

Conclusion

It is mainly in the field of Islamic religious activities that Minazini is most clearly seen as a social unit. Certain activities, notably the annual *Maulid*, and the circumambulation of the village (*kuzingua mji*), are carried out by and on behalf of the whole community. Paradoxically it is also in the same field that the clearest divisions in the society emerge—between those who attend Friday mosque, and are members of the Minazini Sheikh's *tarika* society, and those who do not attend mosque, and are adherents of the southern Sheikh's society. This division is broadly based on descent group lines, with members of descent group A holding most of the mosque offices, as well as most of the posts in the Minazini Sheikh's society. Members of descent group F, on the other hand, hold no mosque posts, and hardly any of them are members of the Minazini Sheikh's *tarika* society; nor do they attend Friday mosque. Together with the members of descent group E, members of group F do however control almost all the official posts in the society of the southern Sheikh. Members of the other descent groups—B, C, and D—fall somewhere in between these two 'extremes'.

Thus the field of Islamic religious activities concerns all those models of society mentioned at the beginning of this chapter—the cognatic descent groups, the 'tribes' of Pokomo and Mbwera, and the socio-religious hierarchy. Indeed, except heuristically these three models cannot be separated, certainly not by the villagers, and even for the outside observer it is plain that the dynamism of the system comes from their interaction.

CHAPTER 6

THE SOCIO-RELIGIOUS HIERARCHY:
(2) SPIRIT POSSESSION

In this chapter the relationship between the descent groups and the socio-religious hierarchy in Minazini is further explored by a consideration of spirit possession activities.[1] Spirit possession in this society is condemned by pious Muslims, particularly by the Sheikh, the mosque officials, most of the Koranic teachers, and others of high status, and its practitioners (particularly the leaders of one of the major cults, who are all Pokomo, and descent group F members) are regarded as of low status as a result.[2] Nonetheless spirit possession activities concern a very large number of people in the village, and provide them with a means of coping with such vital problems as sickness and death.

Categories of spirits

Spirits are thought to be everywhere, and they can be of all types—male, female, weak, strong—almost any adjective can be applied to one or other of them. There is a large number of Swahili terms for different categories, mostly derived from the Arabic. For example, there are spirits called *iblisi* and *chanusi*, which live respectively in rivers and on land. These are essentially malevolent, and cause trouble to any human beings who meet up with them. Nothing can be done about them, as they cannot be contacted.

Of greater importance for this discussion are the types of spirit which can be contacted. In Minazini these may be conveniently divided into two types—those of the sea (*majini*, sing. *jini*), and those of the land (*mashaitani*, sing. *shaitani*). The former live in the sea, but their names and wishes can be learned, and offerings can be made to them by floating little boats out to sea. Land spirits, on the other hand, live on dry land, usually in the bush, and their homes or shrines (*mapango*) are known. (*Mapango* literally means 'caves', but this term is applied to all natural features—rocks, trees, pools, etc.—associated with these spirits.) The field spirits already mentioned in Chapter 4 fall into the category of land spirits.

Orthodox Islam does admit the existence of various types of spirits, and sanctions certain methods of dealing with them. Sheikhs (Islamic holy men) are thought to be particularly efficacious in ridding people of spirits which are afflicting them (cf. Lienhardt 1968:50–1). There are variations in the methods sanctioned by various schools of Islam and even by different Sheikhs, but orthodox Islam condemns the active cultivation of relationships with spirits as *shiriki*, or 'setting up a partner' to God, who is indivisible and all-powerful. Thus the cults involving spirit possession and the activities of guilds centred around spirits are condemned by pious Muslims on Mafia.

This last statement needs some slight qualification. Rituals centred around land spirits involve not only possession, but the drinking of blood, which is contrary to Islamic dietary laws. These rituals are very strongly condemned by those in the village who claim to be pious Muslims, particularly the Sheikh and mosque officials and most of the *walim*. Sea spirits, however, are thought in some vague way to be more 'Koranic'. Some informants even implied that while the sea spirits are 'Moslems', land spirits are 'pagans'. However this distinction was never absolute; some sea spirits are thought to be pagans, and some land spirits to be 'really' jinns. On the whole, however, this broad distinction between sea spirits as Moslems, and land spirits as pagans appears to be borne out by the type of ritual practised in each cult. Rituals to propitiate sea spirits or to initiate a person possessed by one into a guild involve features which are also common to orthodox Islamic ritual; these include the use of the Koran, incense, rose-water, and the Arabic language, and the *dhikiri* of the *tarika* described in the last chapter. Thus although the cults of the sea spirits are condemned, they are not as despised as those of the land spirits, and this has important implications, as will be shown.

Since the two types of spirits involve quite different types of ritual and different categories of participants, I shall discuss them separately, beginning with the cults surrounding the land spirits.

Land spirits

Land spirits may be categorized according to various criteria, the most important of which, for the purpose of this chapter, is whether they are possessory or not. Possessory spirits have cults and guilds organized around them. Non-possessory spirits, while they may be important in certain contexts (for example, some of the field spirits already mentioned in Chapter 5 are non-possessory), are believed to impinge much less on the lives of humans.

Both possessory and non-possessory land spirits can be contacted and offerings made to them. These become necessary when a spirit causes illness, either because it is angry with a human, or else because it has been sent by another human (i.e. someone with a certain degree of control over it) to cause harm. This latter is one form of witchcraft (*uchawi*). These spirits are quite amoral; they do not punish people for doing wrong, nor help them because they are 'good'. They hurt those who have offended them or else those who are the enemies of the humans with whom they are on good terms. They help those who give them presents as an inducement, and more particularly those in some kind of relationship with them. Sometimes spirits are thought to act quite capriciously, and to cause illness simply because they do not like the look of a person.

Relations between land spirits and humans

It should first of all be emphasized that the only people in Minazini who have any sort of relationship with land spirits are Pokomo, i.e. members of descent group F, together with a few Pokomo immigrants from other northern villages. Relationships are said to be of four kinds.

First of all, there is what may be called a 'potential' relationship. This is acquired in one of two ways during childhood, and is not chosen by the subject. Many Pokomo inherit a relationship with a spirit, because one of their parents, or perhaps both, had a similar or even a more intense relationship. Some people, whether or not they themselves have a family connection with a spirit, wish to ensure the protection of a child. They therefore take a present to a spirit, either that of the family, or else one with which they 'make a friendship', and invite it to be the guardian (*mlezi*) of the child, which thus becomes the ward (*kengeja*) of the spirit. If there is already a family connection with a spirit, then it is thought to be dangerous not to ask the spirit to be the child's guardian, as it might be very offended.

On reaching adulthood a person who has a potential relationship may activate it in a number of ways, and may then have what can be termed a 'limited' relationship. This is really a continuation of the childhood relationship, with the spirit guarding its ward, and the ward, in turn, taking offerings to the spirit (of course, when the ward is still a child offerings are taken by the parents). This limited relationship does not involve possession, or membership of a guild, but some people do cultivate the spirit very assiduously, and claim to be able to communicate with it in their dreams. On the other hand, many people completely neglect the guardian spirit of their childhood until a bout of sickness sends them to a diviner, who will remind them of their relationship. Even at this late stage, a 'potential' relationship can be turned into a 'limited' one.

A large proportion of the Pokomo population has a potential relationship with a land spirit. Some of these people also have a limited relationship, although it is difficult to give any precise estimate of their numbers. Potential and limited relationships are held with both possessory and non-possessory spirits. Three group F shrine Guardians, for example, have limited relationships with field spirits which are non-possessory (cf. Chapter 4).

However eight of the ten land spirits in Minazini and most of the other non-Minazini spirits which affect village people (there are about fifteen) are possessory.

Obviously non-possessory spirits cannot enter into the third type of relationship, which is that of *possession*. By this I mean 'a form of trance in which behaviour actions of a person are interpreted as evidence of a control of his behaviour by a spirit normally external to him (Firth 1959b:141). In Swahili the spirit is said to 'climb into the head' (*kupanda kichwani*), and to use the subject as its 'chair' (*kiti chake*). In nearly every case a man or woman is possessed by a spirit with whom there was already a potential, or even a limited, relationship. People just shrug their shoulders and say: 'It is their ancestry' (*asili yao tu*).

Possession (*kusikiwa*) is manifested by various kinds of abnormal behaviour, such as running off into the bush, hysterics (*kupiga kilele*), trance, distorted speech, etc. However a distinction is made between true possession and mere hysteria. The former can only be verified by a shaman, who tries to cause the spirit to 'mount into the subject's head', and say its name and what it wants. On many occasions the first signs of possession are sickness, and trance is not manifested until the process of curing is well under way.

Possession, once ascertained, involves going through a ritual to propitiate the spirit (*kupungwa*) which also makes the subject a member of a guild, and a follower (*mteja*) of the shaman controlling the spirit. The guild member now has certain obligations—i.e. to attend the guild rituals, and is also liable to have the possessory spirit demand that he or she make an offering, or bear the expense of an occasional ritual.

The fourth type of relationship with a spirit is that of *shamanism*[3], which implies some degree of control over a spirit. Shamans of land spirits can induce possession at will, and are thought to be able to manipulate the spirit to give them information (e.g. in divination or curing), to help cure a sick person, to cause illness in an enemy or the enemy of a client, and generally to protect the shamans themselves. Shamans are thus feared by many people, because they are witches, doctors, and diviners. They can be both men and women, and inherit their status through either parent, but it is most common to succeed a father or paternal grandfather. There are ten male land spirit shamans in Minazini, and only one woman.

Shamans are paid for their services, and also receive a fee 'for the spirit', usually in the form of a cow. Some of them thus build up large herds, which nominally belong to their possessory spirits, but to which they have access. Two Minazini shamans are extremely wealthy men, each controlling herds of over 50 cattle, in addition to owning coconut trees and donkeys. The majority of other land spirit shamans are heads of households which are either 'viable' or 'surplus'. Furthermore, as leaders of guilds they have prestige and influence not only among their own followers but outside the guilds as well.

Cults and guilds

A cult is defined as being centred upon a certain category of spirits, and using a particular type of ritual. It may be practised by several guilds. There are two cults of land spirits in the village, called *kitanga* and *mwingo*; these are the names of both the cult and the type of dance ritual practised by the cult adherents. The *kitanga* is the main cult in Minazini, and is also practised in two other northern villages, while the *mwingo* cult is relatively unimportant in Minazini, but is the chief cult in three other northern villages. The rituals associated with the cults have a lot in common; in fact the main difference is in the use of the drum in *kitanga* rituals, whereas only hand-clapping is allowed in *mwingo* rituals. In most other essential features they are the same. Most of the discussion about land spirit cults in this chapter concerns *kitanga* guilds.

A guild (*kilinge*) is composed of men and women who have been possessed by the same spirit, under the leadership of the shaman who controls the spirit, and gives the guild its name. Normally guild rituals are held at the house of the shaman. There are four categories of people associated with guilds. First of all, there are those who are not possessed, and cannot strictly be called members; these I have termed *assistants*, since they help with practical matters. They herd cattle which belong to the spirit of the guild, help to keep the shaman's house (which he is said to share with the spirit) in good repair, and on the occasion of rituals perform any odd jobs that need doing. They are almost invariably very close relatives of the shaman.

Secondly, there are *ordinary guild members*, men and women, whose functions have already been discussed in the section on possession. A few of these members, however, do reach the position of *senior members*, and play a significant part in organizing rituals and assisting the shamans. Both men and women can be senior members, although women tend to outnumber men. Finally, there are the *shamans* themselves.

There are four *kitanga* guilds in Minazini. Two centre around spirits from other northern villages whence the shamans of these guilds originally came; many of the members trace descent in these villages. The two larger guilds are both based in ward F, and they are the only two guilds which have senior members and other assistants. I shall refer to these two guilds as group F, guilds 1 and 2. Normally, each guild consists of a shaman and his followers, but in the largest guild, that of group F, guild 1, there are no fewer than four shamans, one of whom is the woman already mentioned.

The following table shows the relative sizes of the four *kitanga* guilds in Minazini, and the status of those attached to them:

TABLE 27
Kitanga guilds: size, and status of members

Grade	Group F guilds		Outside guilds		Others*	Total
	1	2	1	2		
Shamans	4	1	1	1	—	
Senior members	2	1	—	—	—	
Ordinary members	13	13	5	8	8	
Assistants	2	—	—	—	—	
	21	15	6	9	8	59

Note: * These are people who are members of guilds based in other northern villages.

As the foregoing table shows, some 59 men and women are directly involved with guilds, or 15 per cent of the adult population. However the guilds and their activities affect a much larger proportion of the population because most of them concern sickness.

Activities of guilds

The *raison d'être* of the guilds is said by Minazini people to be the diagnosis, curing, and prevention of sickness, both physical and mental. In the course of achieving this, the guilds recruit new members and gain animals and cash. Members have an opportunity not afforded them elsewhere for certain psychological satisfactions, and the shamans, or at least those who are successful, increase their prestige and their wealth.

Life in Minazini is a hazardous business, particularly in the early years. Almost as many children die before the age of fifteen as reach adulthood. Various explanations are advanced by people living in Minazini for these sicknesses and deaths.

(a) Ancestors are believed to be capable of causing illness, but not death, in order to draw attention to themselves. They usually make a small child sick, because they want him or her as a namesake (*somo*) (cf. Chapter 3). In such cases the child's name may be changed to that of the ancestor who has thus indicated his or her wishes. Occasionally the child's *somo* makes him or her sick because he feels neglected. The remedy here is to hold a Koranic reading (*hitima*) on the grave of the *somo*.

(b) Another explanation of sickness, and more particularly, general misfortune in adult life, is that a parent has withdrawn his or her 'satisfaction before God' (*radhi*) with the child. This may be likened to a parental curse, and the effect is to prevent anything the child does from prospering. The form of the curse is often, 'may your life, as long as you live, be like a coconut shell with holes in it', or else, 'may you live as if you were not living'. Sometimes the angry parent can be persuaded to 'reinstate' the child, but often the parent dies before this is done.

(c) Illness is sometimes attributed to natural causes such as old age, the will of God, or 'bad luck'.

(d) It is believed that illness and even death can be caused by the activities of land spirits. There are three reasons for a land spirit to harm someone: firstly because it is angry, perhaps that a debt has not been paid for help given in the past, or else a human has infringed one of the rules for dealing with spirits, e.g. humans should not come into contact with spirits when 'dirty' from semen or menstrual blood; secondly because the spirit wishes to possess the sick person, and chooses this way of drawing attention to itself; or finally because someone with control over the spirit has sent it to hurt or kill an enemy.

The most important method of determining which of the above explanations is correct in any set of circumstances is by divination, which is of two types. One is through a 'Koranic' diviner, usually a *mwalim*, who uses figures in the sand (*kupiga ramli*) or astrology (*kupiga falaki*). The second is to consult a shaman at a time when he is possessed by his spirit (this type of divination is called *kutazamia*). All land spirit shamans can act as diviners, and most of them do so on occasion. However, a virtual monopoly of this type of divination in Minazini is held by one of the shamans of the largest guild, that of group F, guild 1, who has a wide reputation in northern Mafia.

The very choice of diviner determines to some extent the type of explanation given, for the shaman diviner nearly always explains illness in terms of the activities of spirits, whereas a Koranic diviner uses a wider range of explanation, including the anger of an ancestor wanting a namesake or a Koranic reading, or the will of God. In certain circumstances, however, he may attribute it to the action of a spirit (see Case 12).

What determines the choice of diviner? To some extent this is purely practical; in early 1966, there were two men regularly practising as diviners—one was the shaman diviner of group F, guild 1, and the other was a *mwalim*. Later that year the latter went to live in Zanzibar. Thus people who wished to consult a Koranic diviner would have had to go to another village and so many people who might formerly have consulted a Koranic diviner tended to consult the shaman diviner instead.

However the most important consideration is ancestry. The shaman diviner is consulted by people who are of Pokomo descent; he is hardly ever consulted by people who have no Pokomo descent, i.e. are of 'pure' Mbwera, Gunya, or slave descent. During my attendances at the divination sessions of this man, I saw 23 Minazini people ask him for information—there were others who had come from various northern villages—and only two of these were not Pokomo; one of the two was an immigrant from Kilwa.

It should be remembered at this stage that half of the adult population in the village can be categorized as Pokomo, since 222 adults are members of the F descent group, and a handful of others are immigrants from other villages. Many of these Pokomo are also Mbwera, that is they have mixed descent, and a minority of this category stress only their affiliations with Mbwera descent groups for status reasons, and would never consult the shaman diviner. But the majority of people with any Pokomo descent do consult him, and he is often able to explain their sickness in terms of the action of spirits for two reasons. First of all, many Pokomo inherit a potential relationship with a land spirit through their Pokomo forebears. Secondly, because the F descent group controls the majority of bush land in the village, nearly everyone who is of F group descent uses this membership to obtain land at some time or other. As I explained in Chapter 4, most F group land is associated with field spirits, and certain specific rules have to be obeyed by people cultivating such land. The shaman diviner, who knows of course which people have cultivated such land (since he himself is a field Guardian, and allocates much of it), can nearly always find an explanation in terms of misbehaviour while in the fields. The following case gives an example of this:

CASE II

A field spirit punishes quarrelsome women

Binti Hatibu and Binti Athman were both cultivating group F fields, controlled by a field spirit. The two women quarrelled violently during the course of the agricultural season, when they were living out in the fields.

Subsequently both women became sick, and the explanation given by the shaman diviner was that they had annoyed the spirit by shouting at each other in its 'town'.

Apparently Binti Hatibu was thought by the shaman to be more blameworthy, and he ordered her to pay half the cost of a cow. She did do, and recovered. Binti Athman was told to pay the spirit only the cost of a tray of sweetmeats[4], but she failed to find the money. However, she later recovered.

Some time later, when Binti Athman was again cultivating the field of the same spirit, she fell sick. The diviner reminded her of her debt to the spirit and this time she paid up.

As this case illustrates, not only can a single case of illness be explained in terms of the action of a spirit, but frequently several cases of illness. The reason is that offerings to the spirits tend to be extremely expensive, and people delay paying their debts. The diviner meanwhile can continually use this unpaid debt to the spirit as an explanation for the sickness either of the debtor himself, or of his immediate family.

Because of the high proportion of the population which is involved in some way with spirits, through descent and/or cultivation of F group fields, many cases of illness are attributed to the action of spirits. I kept a record of all cases of illness and death which came to my attention during my stay in the village. No fewer than 77 per cent (57 cases out of 74) were attributed to the action of a spirit. This statement needs qualifying in two respects. Firstly, there may have been some bias in my record taking, because frequently it was at a divination session that my attention was drawn to a particular case of illness. Secondly, in several cases included in the above figures, more than one explanation was advanced, at different stages in the illness, and by different people. Thus it is quite common for people to consult the shaman diviner, and to follow whatever line of action he recommends, and also to consult a Koranic diviner, the village dispenser, or the hospital in Kilindoni, and indeed any other kind of practitioner available. The fact remains however that in the majority of cases one of the explanations advanced for illness or death is the action of a spirit.

Of course those people who are involved in spirit possession would be much more likely to use a spirit as a source of explanation, whereas people of high religious status would say that sickness is caused by the will of God or 'bad luck', and scoff at the former type of explanation as 'foolishness and ignorance'. But those people who give no credence at all to spirit explanations are in a minority.

Even if the diviner does not diagnose the activities of a spirit, he usually recommends his clients to one of the shamans in the village, or may undertake treatment himself, because shamans control most of the remedies for sickness, apart from those provided by the government dispensary. During the course of treatment for illness, shamans often encourage their clients to become possessed, because this means that they will have to be initiated into a guild.

Initiation of a man or woman into a guild is through the holding of the appropriate dance ritual (*ngoma*). Guild members dance and sing all night to invoke the spirits, and in the morning, when all are possessed, including the initiate, a cow or bullock is slaughtered, and first the initiate, and then the shaman, followed by other shamans and guild members, drink its blood.

Such a ritual, which costs in the region of 250s., is paid for by the initiate and his or her relatives. Not surprisingly many people have their troubles diagnosed as possession by a spirit, but are unable to afford to be initiated for some time. Nor do expenses end with initiation, as frequently guild members are told by their shamans to provide an animal for slaughter, or at least a tray of sweetmeats as an offering to the spirit. Having once become a member of a guild, a man or woman is influenced to a large degree by the shaman who leads the guild, and can usually be induced to find the necessary cash for such offerings.

Possession and descent group membership

As has already been stressed, people who are possessed by land spirits are almost invariably Pokomo. However they can be divided into two categories: those who are 'pure' Pokomo, and those who are part Pokomo, part Mbwera. Only a minority of the latter category participates in guild activities, although many others seek help from shamans on occasion.

The people most closely involved in spirit possession activities, particularly shamans and senior guild members, usually fall into the former category. There are ten shamans and senior members of the *kitanga* guilds; only four of them have any Mbwera descent at all, and all of these have only one grandparent who was not a member of descent group F. The reason for this is that there is a high degree of intra-marriage among such people, and an endogamous subgroup has been formed within the larger F descent group.

What are the reasons for this very high degree of intra-marriage? One is that it accords with the general preference for marriage between close kin, which has already been discussed in Chapter 2. More often however it seems likely that parents who are themselves deeply involved in possession cults are likely to marry their children off to people with whom they interact in this context. Such marriages may also be seen to cement ties between shamans and their closest followers.

There is another reason for the high degree of intra-marriage between people who practise spirit possession—it constitutes a reaction to the discriminatory marriage practices of those with high status (cf. Chapter 7). Undoubtedly, spirit possession practitioners find it difficult to marry women from Mbwera descent groups, and an Mbwera man, especially a pious one, would also probably not wish to marry a woman from a family known to be involved in possession cults. But people who are Pokomo and not highly involved in spirit possession activities are also unwilling to marry those who are. Such people will of course find it easier to marry Mbwera, if they wish to do so. This leads to a positing of status differentials within the F descent group between those who practise spirit possession and those who do not, which is very often coincident with the distinction first made at the beginning of this section between those who are 'pure' Pokomo and those who are 'mixed' Pokomo and Mbwera.

To what extent then do people choose whether or not to participate in guild activities? Obviously those people who are brought up surrounded by guild activities may have little choice, although not all of them will become possessed. In cases of sickness they will turn to their relatives who are shamans and diviners, who will tell them that they must not neglect the spirits with whom they have inherited relationships. Furthermore those Pokomo people who have no membership of descent groups other than group F are virtually forced to cultivate its land, which brings them again into contact with spirits.

People who have both Mbwera and Pokomo descent have a greater choice. They may use both sets of affiliations when it suits them. They may participate in spirit possession cults in a limited way (e.g. for curing, divination, etc.) and at the same time participate in 'Islamic' activities. A good example is provided by the following case:

CASE 12

Sickness of a small boy

The two-year old son of a Minazini woman became sick. This woman is a member of descent groups A, B, E, and F. She consulted an Islamic diviner, and he said that because she had not 'said farewell' to the land spirit with which she had inherited a relationship, when she made a trip away from Minazini, it had become angry and made her son ill.

She therefore went to the shaman of the spirit concerned and through him made an offering of a tray of sweetmeats to the spirit.

This woman lives in an A group ward (that of the Crossroads), and participates in many orthodox Islamic rituals; she is also a member of the Minazini Sheikh's *tarika*. In this instance of her son's illness, she consulted a Koranic diviner, but he, perhaps at her suggestion, stressed her Pokomo (group F) membership in giving his explanation. She accepted this in taking an offering to the land spirit.

However, other people of mixed Pokomo–Mbwera descent may totally ignore their Pokomo descent, and stress only their membership of Mbwera descent groups. They may even join with other pious Mbwera in condemning spirit possession activities, and will never consult a shaman. Other Pokomo say of them, and of all who profess to scoff at spirit possession, that they secretly believe in the efficacy of spirit cures, and consult shamans in private. It is interesting to note that even full siblings, who share the same sets of descent links, may stress ties with quite different groups, particularly in the context of Islam and spirit possession. The following case, not an isolated example by any means, demonstrates this:

CASE 13

Different approaches to sickness

J.M. and A.M. are two full brothers living in the same cluster of the F group ward (cf. Chapter 3, Fig. 5). Their father was a member of groups B and F and their mother a B group woman, a member of the segment now living in the southern ward which associates with group A and people of high socio-religious status.

J.M. is highly religious, attends mosque regularly, and even walks to Kirongwe once a week for advanced Koranic classes. When he is sick, he uses Koranic charms, cupping, and goes to the dispensary; he occasionally uses herbal medicines, but never consults a shaman.

A.M., on the other hand, consults the head of his cluster, his father's brother (who is a *mwingo* shaman) and other shamans for remedies. He also believes in witchcraft, and he attends spirit possession rituals regularly, although he is not a member of a guild, and has a limited relationship with a land spirit. A.M. does not attend mosque, and identifies more closely with group F than with the B descent group.

Sea spirits

Sea spirits cannot be categorized as conveniently as can land spirits, one reason being that most of them are not even named. However they are sometimes classed into 'tribes'—the commonest are called Subhani, Rohani, Bedu, Hambali, and Katani. Like land spirits sea spirits are both possessory and non-possessory; the latter are called *Mabwengu*.[5]

Relations between sea spirits and humans

Relationships between humans and sea spirits are not inherited in the same way as they are with land spirits, nor are relationships with them confined to a category defined by descent. Members of all descent groups in Minazini are possessed by sea spirits, but here a different categorization becomes important—that of sex. Sea spirit cults are essentially women's cults,[6] and they concern women's problems, such as marriage, frigidity, fertility, and pregnancy.

The majority of sea spirits in Minazini are thought to be 'love spirits' (*majini ya mahaba*). A woman may acquire a love spirit when she is still quite young, and it can remain with her after she reaches puberty and marries. This spirit is believed to be like a husband to her, so that she gets no satisfaction from sexual relationships with human men. Furthermore, sea spirits, like land spirits, dislike sexual 'dirt', particularly that caused by semen or childbirth. They are thus said not only to try to prevent a woman from having sexual relations with a man by making her frigid, but also to render her sterile, or cause her to miscarry, or cause a newly born child to die.

Some women become possessed by sea spirits, and then are initiated into a guild. Initiation is regarded as the chief way of curing a large number of lost pregnancies or sterility, as a bargain is struck with the spirit, and it 'agrees' to let the woman bear children in return for presents. The spirit is also made the guardian of the child, in the same way as are land spirits, but in fact sea spirits are not thought to be as effective in protecting children, and the relationship between spirit and ward does not last beyond childhood.

A few men are also possessed by sea spirits, but these are all shamans or else apprentice shamans. It is notable however that not all sea spirit shamans are possessed; some are able to control spirits through their knowledge of Arabic books on astrology and magic. However sea spirit shamans are not as feared as the shamans of land spirits, because they are not thought to be able to cause sickness and death.

Cults and guilds

A sea spirit cult is defined in the same way as is a land spirit cult—it is differentiated by a particular kind of ritual. There are two cults which affect the villagers: the *mkobero*, which is practised widely in Minazini and another northern village, and the *tari*, which is confined to a third northern village. The other northern villages have no sea spirit cults, probably because they are all inland villages. In this discussion, I shall be describing only the *mkobero* cult as practised in Minazini.

There are three *mkobero* guilds in Minazini. Their organization differs somewhat from that of the *kitanga* guilds already described. The assistants attached to the guild are of two kinds: there are helpers who assist with practical matters, and there are also men who can read the Koran, which is required for the rituals of these guilds. Both shamans and senior members are to be found in *mkobero* guilds, and there is in addition a category of apprentice shamans. *Mkobero* shamans are not recruited in quite the same way as *kitanga* and *mwingo* shamans; they spend some time with a practising shaman 'learning the job', and they may or may not inherit the post of shaman from a father or grandfather. Furthermore, as already stated, they are not usually possessed by the spirit which they control, as are the land spirit shamans.

The following table shows the relative sizes of *mkobero* guilds in Minazini:

TABLE 28
Mkobero guilds: size and status of members

Grades	Bakari (E group ward)	Hamis (A group ward)	Jumbe (F group ward)	Total
Shamans	(2)	I	(I)	1 + (3)
Apprentices	2 + (I)	1 + (2)	I + (I)	4 + (4)
Senior members	2 + (I)	I	—	3 + (I)
Ordinary members	10	16	17	43
Total in Minazini	14	19	18	51
Total outside Minazini	(4)	(2)	(2)	(8)

Note: Figures in brackets refer to people living outside Minazini.

The largest guild is that of Hamis, with a total of 21 members; two apprentices live outside Minazini. The only men in the guild are the shaman and three apprentices, one of whom is the shaman's sister's son. The latter's mother is the senior member. This guild has its headquarters in the A group ward, although not all the rituals necessarily take place there. Few of its members are A group women, the majority being members of groups C and D, with a few women from group F. Three rituals were held in 1966, and one woman was initiated.

Jumbe's guild is almost as large, with 20 members, two of whom live outside the village; these are the shaman himself and one of the apprentice shamans. The former is in fact one of the most famous shamans in Mafia, as he is thought to control both a land spirit, which possesses him, and sea spirits. He is a Minazini man of the F descent group, and has spent much of his youth and early manhood serving as a soldier. He claims to have visited Egypt and the Middle East, and to have acquired his knowledge of Islamic magic and astrology during the course of his travels. Whatever the truth of his stories, most people think that he is very powerful, and are much afraid of him. It is probable that he has many more *mkobero* adherents than those shown in the foregoing table, which shows only those ordinary members who live in Minazini, and take part in the activities of the guild located in the F group ward, where Jumbe's brother lives.

Some of the members of this guild are F group women, but there are also women from the B descent group. Only one ritual was held by this guild in 1966, and this was an offering for a child which had learned to walk.[7] However, in the course of the ritual several other women went through the first stages of initiation (see below), and some who were already guild members made offerings.

The third guild, that of Bakari, is situated in the E group ward, and, more than any other, this guild is a close knit kinship unit in spite of the fact that the two shamans, who are brothers, both live away from Minazini, as does one of the apprentices and a senior guild member, as well as some of the ordinary members. Very few of the members of this guild are not E group people or women married to E group men (cf. Fig. 12, p. 116).

Three rituals were held by this guild in 1966. Three new women members were initiated, and three others gave offerings. All of the rituals of this guild are held in the E group's ward, in the same place as the rituals of the *tarika*, and indeed, many of those prominent in the guild are closely related to officials of the *tarika*, as Fig. 12 shows. There might seem to be a contradiction here between spirit possession activities which are regarded as unlawful (*haramu*) by pious Muslims, and *tarika* society activities whose ostensible purpose is 'the glorification of God'. Two explanations are advanced by Group E people who are involved in both; they point out that sea spirit possession is not as 'bad' (*upotevu*) as land spirit possession. Furthermore, Bakari's guild, unlike the other two *mkobero* guilds, does not slaughter animals nor drink blood during its rituals.

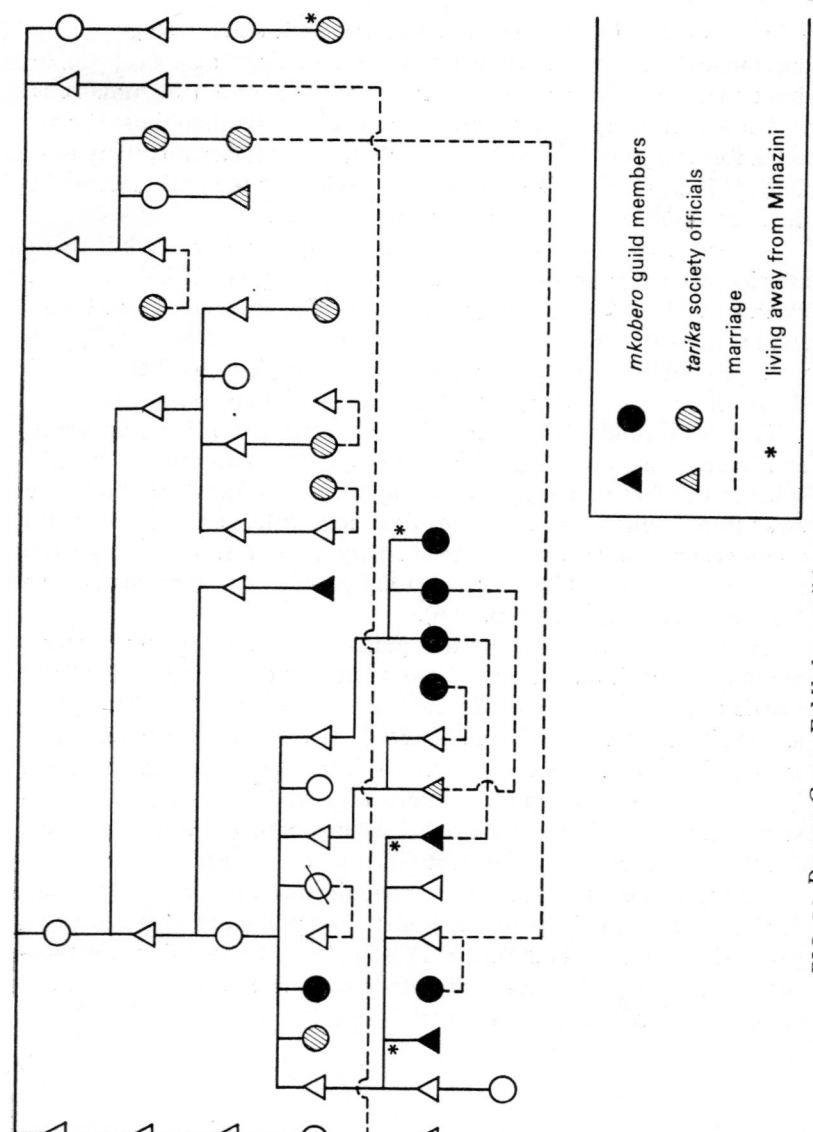

FIG. 12 *Descent Group E Mkobero* guild members and *tarika* society officials

Activities of guilds

The primary purpose of the *mkobero* guilds is to help women to come to terms with problems arising from their sex. People usually suspect that a woman is being troubled by a sea spirit if she fails in her role as a wife and mother. She may also become hysterical and run off to the sea-shore. In such cases her relatives take her to a Koranic diviner or to a shaman who will attempt to make the spirit possess her, speak its name, and say what it wants. Only then is it possible to come to some arrangement with the spirit, whereby the woman is allowed to function normally, in return for her becoming a guild member, and making frequent presents to the spirit.

It is noticeable that many women become hysterical or possessed for the first time in stress situations. Young girls may appear to become possessed at the time of their first marriage, particularly when they are married off to men living in other villages, as the following case shows:

CASE 14

A young wife is unhappy, and sea-spirit possession is suspected

Binti A. was married off at puberty to a distant relative in a village in central Mafia, which is some four hours' walk from Minazini. Her parents were unable to visit her, as her father's health was poor, and her mother had a deformed foot.

After a short time her husband brought her back to her parents, and said that she was sick. She remained in her parents' house, while her husband returned to his own village. She constantly became hysterical and ran off to the sea-shore, pursued by relatives who brought her back and attempted to calm her down. They took her to various shamans and it was decided that a sea spirit was troubling her.

During the course of a *mkobero* ritual Binti A. offered a tray of sweetmeats to the spirit, but she failed to become possessed. Soon afterwards however her husband divorced her, and she remained in Minazini with her parents. Some time later she married a Minazini man.

If the woman is frigid, or refuses to have sexual relations with her husband, she is very likely to exhibit the symptoms mentioned above. Sex is considered a normal and pleasurable activity for both men and women and sexual instruction plays an important part in a girl's puberty rites (cf. Caplan *in the press*). Women who are frigid are said either to be 'sick' or else they are thought to be afflicted by a spirit.

Likewise, if a woman fails to bear children, or else if she loses most of her children while they are babies, the explanation is usually made that a sea spirit is preventing her from having children. This again may be a point where she becomes possessed and is initiated into a guild as part of her treatment.

On the other hand some women who are extremely fertile become possessed after a long series of pregnancies. Usually in such cases they exhibit symptoms of hysteria, and are then sent home to be treated, probably again by initiation into a guild. Undoubtedly women may subconsciously use the excuse of spirit possession to get away from their husbands, or perhaps to force a relative to undertake the upbringing of some of their children.

Another occasion on which a woman is likely to manifest possession symptoms is when her husband takes a second wife. As Lewis (1966 and 1971) has suggested, possession may reassure the wife about her husband's affections, since he has to pay a large part of the costs of initiation into a guild. It is interesting to note in this connection that almost without fail, if one wife of a polygynously married man becomes possessed and is initiated, the other wife follows suit.

There are two categories of treatment: one is to get rid of the spirit altogether, the other is to 'come to terms' with it. The first may be effected either by using a medicine made from a plant called *mavimavi* which is said to smell like human excreta, and prevent the spirit from coming to the woman at night, or else by a Sheikh using Koranic methods and exorcizing the spirit. The second effect is achieved through initiation into a guild.

Initiation

Initiation is usually in two stages. In the first stage the woman (and her relatives) bear the cost of a ritual during which she (i.e. the spirit 'in her head') consumes the offering of a tray of sweetmeats. The second stage in the majority of guilds (not that of Bakari) is when she offers a goat to the spirit and drinks the blood, in rather the same way as do participants in the *kitanga* ritual.

The form of the *mkobero* ritual is quite different from that of the *mwingo* or the *kitanga*. First of all the ritual is usually held on Thursdays, i.e. the day before the Islamic sabbath, and since the ritual usually continues all night, the culmination is on the holy day, Friday. The ritual begins with the initiate, and any other guild members who are making an offering, sitting on a mat, while incense is burned under their noses and the *mwalim* and/or shaman reads from the Koran.

The women are offered rose-water and saffron water to drink, and soon become possessed.

When this happens everyone starts the *dhikiri* of the *tarika* and this continues all night. The form of *dhikiri* and the songs are exactly the same as at a conventional *tarika* ritual. The climax is when the tray of sweetmeats (*sinia*) or the goat is offered to the spirit. Only those who are being or have already been initiated are allowed to consume the food or blood, although others may dance and be possessed during the course of the ritual. This differs from the *kitanga* or *mwingo* rituals, where anyone who is possessed can drink the blood, or eat the sweetmeats, and it emphasizes one of the main differences between these two types of cult. In the cults of the land spirits descent is the most important criterion for recruitment; people can participate even before initiation because they already have potential relationships with the spirit, but the *mkobero* cult has little to do with descent, and only those who choose to be initiated may participate in this way.

Another important difference between the two types of cult is in the language used. For the land spirit cults there is a special 'spirit' vocabulary.[8] In the *mkobero* cult 'Arabic' is the language used by the possessed. As I have already said, the rituals begin with a Koranic reading, which is of course in Arabic. The first signs of possession are when a woman gives the Arabic greeting normally only used by males in this society—'Salaam aleikum'. The rest of the ritual is also conducted in 'Arabic'. In actual fact hardly anyone in the village is able to understand the Koran, much less hold a conversation in Arabic. However since they all hear Arabic frequently when the Koran is read, they know what it (Arabic) is supposed to sound like. Hence a series of Arabic-like sounds passes for the real thing and people marvel all the more that women, most of whom are not able to read the Koran or recite prayers, when possessed speak 'Arabic' so fluently.

This reflects another aspect of this spirit possession cult. The sea spirits are described as being 'fair, like Arabs' and 'very handsome'. The articles in use in the rituals—incense, rose-water, cordial, dates, etc.—are all associated with Arabs, who constitute a large proportion of shopkeepers on the coast. In both land spirit and sea spirit rituals, trays of sweetmeats are offered; in the former cults, these are called '*chano*', which means a wooden locally made tray, whereas those given to the sea spirits are '*sinia*', manufactured metal trays obtained only in shops. The implication here is that the land spirits dislike manufactured articles,[9] whereas the sea spirits like only 'things of shops', or 'Arab things', the two being synonymous in this culture. The importance of emulating Arabs, already referred to earlier, is thus symbolized in the sea spirit possession cult.

Economics of initiation

Initiation into a *mkobero* guild is not as expensive as into a *kitanga* guild, mainly because cows cost more money than goats (150s.–250s. as opposed to 50s.–75s.), and in any case goats are not always used in initiation, particularly in Bakari's guild. Thus a woman has only to find the cost of a tray of sweetmeats, a set of new clothes, the 'things of the shop' (incense, rose-water, etc.) and possibly a meal before the ritual is held. Even the last is not mandatory, as some rituals are not all-night affairs, like the *kitanga* rituals. In short, the total maximum cost of initiation is in the region of 150s., and this is assuming that the initiate buys both a goat and a tray of sweetmeats, which is not usual. Some women are initiated in two stages, first with a tray, then with a goat, but others use a goat immediately, and any trays offered are usually given by other women who wish to make a present to the spirit for various reasons. Women can raise this money with the help of husbands and kin and by selling mats or even trees.

Sea spirit guilds and shamans are not wealthy as are some of the *kitanga* guilds and shamans. The reason for this is that they do not undertake divination and curing of general sickness in the same way as do shamans of the land spirits. Nor are offerings, other than those consumed during the course of a ritual, made to any particular spirit. This means that herds of animals are not built up from the fees for curing given to sea spirits, as is the case with land spirits. It is difficult to judge the wealth of the sea spirit shamans, as several of them are not resident in Minazini. Jumbe who lives in a neighbouring village is probably one of the wealthiest shamans in Mafia, but he is also a land spirit shaman, and undertakes a large amount of divination and curing. He is also a successful trader. On the other hand, Hamis, the shaman of the guild with the largest number of Minazini members, is not a rich man by any standards, and indeed spends most of his time herding other people's cows, an occupation which is considered fit only for the simple-minded or the very poor.

Spirit possession: discussion

Why do people become possessed by spirits? And why is it that only certain categories become possessed, that is, women in the case of sea spirits, and Pokomo in the case of land spirits? Lewis (1966, 1970, 1971) has discussed possible sociological approaches to the phenomenon of spirit possession and has stressed that those most commonly possessed are the socially 'deprived', particularly women in male-dominated societies, or occasionally men of low social status. He has also maintained that spirit possession is a weapon in the 'sex war'.

Wilson (1967) appears to accept Lewis's premise that the majority of people possessed are women, but he has argued that the reason for this is that they frequently suffer from 'status ambiguity', and use spirit possession more clearly to define their roles or create new ones. He rejects the idea that spirit possession is a weapon in 'the war between the sexes', and suggests instead that spirit possession is used in situations of competition between members of the same sex.

Although the epithet 'downtrodden' which Lewis (1966) applies to Somali women is not a very suitable one for north Mafia women, who in many respects are much less oppressed than women in other Islamic societies, nonetheless there is no doubt that women suffer disadvantages, in both the domestic and public spheres in comparison with men. Women are more likely to have to change their residence upon marriage, and this may involve moving to another village. They are more likely to be divorced than to initiate divorce proceedings. Women may also feel threatened if their husbands wish to take second wives. And, as in most societies, the problems and difficulties of childbirth and child-rearing tend to fall more heavily upon their shoulders than upon those of their husbands, although in this society men do participate to a large extent in child-rearing, and women also receive help from their parents, husbands' parents, and possibly from their own or their husbands' siblings.

Economically women are less well off than men, with a smaller amount of capital in the form of coconut trees per head; they have fewer opportunities of acquiring capital because of the inheritance ratio, and because they rarely have cash with which to buy. Methods of earning cash which are open to men (trading, fishing, labouring, etc.) are not open to women.

In the public sector women play little overt part in the most important Islamic institution—the Friday mosque—although some of them go to Koran schools, and there are as many women *tarika* officials as men. Women do not attend public meetings, or play any overt role in politics, although they are frequently active in disputes and may engage in politics by indirect means, e.g. the singing of songs concerning disputes and village politics at feasts. Women also play a very important role in organizing rites of passage.

It can then perhaps be argued that women suffer from 'status ambiguity' in the marital sphere, particularly when first married, or divorced, or threatened by a co-wife. It is also true that they are relatively excluded from certain Islamic and political spheres. Even so it can scarcely be said that the *mkobero* cult provides them with a substitute, for in fact the guilds of this cult are led by male shamans, and thus do not provide avenues for women to achieve leadership roles.

However this latter explanation may be more appropriate for the cult of land spirits, in which only the Pokomo participate. There is undoubtedly a correlation between the fact that so few Pokomo participate, much less hold office, in the religious and political fields, and the fact that they dominate the land spirit cults. Given the monopoly in religious and political affairs which the Mbwera and Gunya enjoy, it is not surprising that the Pokomo seek a substitute activity. Of course they are not barred from participation in mosque affairs, nor from attending village council meetings, but the point is that, until very recently, they would be extremely unlikely to become office-holders in these fields (cf. Chapter 7).

In the context of land spirit possession, on the other hand, the Pokomo, or some of them at any rate, can achieve very real power and wealth.[10] Many of the land spirit shamans in Minazini are fairly rich by local standards; two of the *kitanga* shamans in particular are among the richest men in the village, vying with people of high status such as the Sheikh. Apart from fees for curing people, they also receive fees 'on behalf of the spirit', and in this way can build up herds of cattle and stores of money. The shaman has almost unrestricted access to this wealth, although officially he can only 'borrow' from the spirit. He can also borrow money on the strength of this wealth, because in the eyes of the government officials from Kilindoni he is the owner. Even those shamans who are less successful fall into the category of those men who have a surplus of cash over expenditure, or at least who have sufficient cash to meet their needs. Only a very few shamans fall into the economic category of those who do not have enough cash to meet their needs, and these are all *mwingo* shamans, who in Minazini are eclipsed by the more successful *kitanga* shamans.

In addition to their economic status shamans have a large amount of control over the actions of their adherents, particularly guild members. They can put pressure on people to follow a certain course of action; for example, a shaman's attitude towards his patient, particularly if female, may decide whether or not she returns to her husband after curing, or demands a divorce.[11] An additional fringe benefit for shamans is the number of opportunities for sexual relations with female patients presented during the course of curative treatment.

Shamans enjoy a large amount of prestige not only among their own adherents, but even further afield. One *kitanga* shaman has patients who come from the mainland coast, as well as other parts of Mafia. Even people who are considered to be unsympathetic towards the activities of shamans (e.g. pious Muslims) accord a certain grudging respect to some of the more famous ones, although they disapprove of their methods of curing people.

Apart from the shamans, ordinary guild members in both types of cult obviously derive considerable psychological satisfaction from their participation. The rituals are highly 'theatrical', and exciting to watch. Dancers can behave in an uninhibited way which is not normally tolerated; difficulties and fears can be voiced without shame, and reassurance given by relatives, fellow guild members, and shamans.

Conclusion

In sum, then, spirit possession in Minazini highlights two important cleavages in the society. Firstly, there is the cleavage between men and women. To the extent that some women, at least, suffer from problems concerning their marriages or their fertility, they can find in sea spirit possession cults relief which they cannot get elsewhere.

The possession cults associated with land spirits, on the other hand, express the division between the Mbwera (group A in particular) and Pokomo (mainly group F members) within the society. In the sense that the members of group A and the Gunya dominate the 'legitimate' or most highly valued offices, group F's leadership of land spirit possession cults and guilds can be viewed as a response to deprivation or exclusion from positions demanding high socio-religious status. Alternatively, of course, it can be argued that the benefits accruing from participation in these cults—the explanations they provide for misfortune and the economic advantages available to the leaders—are sufficient inducements in themselves, and are seen by some F group members as a positive alternative to orthodox religion and politics.

CHAPTER 7

THE HIERARCHY AND VILLAGE POLITICS

The socio-religious hierarchy discussed in the last two chapters concerns not only Islamic and spirit possession activities; it also has important political implications. In Minazini power tends to flow from high status, and as a result most of the positions of political power are occupied by the same people as occupy positions of power in the orthodox Islamic institutions—mosque, *tarika* (particularly that of the Minazini Sheikh) and Koran schools. In this chapter I want to discuss not only this fact, but also the way in which people of high status use marriage both to maintain that status and as a political strategy.

Administration

The present political system has been in operation only since just after the time of Independence in 1961. Prior to this each village was led by a Headman (*Jumbe*) who had to be approved by the (European) District Commissioner. The Headman was responsible for law and order and seeing that taxes were paid. He also held a court at which minor offences and disputes were dealt with, and in this latter task he was assisted by a Council of Elders (*wazee*).

Since 1961 Mafia Island has constituted a separate District of the Coastal Region of Tanzania, and is also a single parliamentary constituency. It is divided for administrative purposes into two Divisions, based on Kirongwe and Utende villages; each Division is administered by a Divisional Executive Officer (DEO), who is appointed by the District Council.

The island is also sub-divided into seventeen administrative villages, each of which sends a representative to the Mafia District Council. The Council representatives (*madiwani*, sing. *diwani*) are elected directly by the villagers, and in addition a handful of extra members are co-opted by the Council. The District Council has responsibility for primary schools, village dispensaries, and upkeep of roads. It is financed by local rates (30s. per annum paid by every able-bodied adult male), licences for radios, for shops, and for bicycles, and central government grants.

The Council also selects and pays Village Executive Officers (VEOs), who are posted to the villages. Their job is to encourage self-help schemes, and generally to assist in administration. At the time of fieldwork, there were VEOs in only seven of the seventeen villages, one of which was Minazini; the VEO posted in Minazini also had responsibility for two neighbouring northern villages. Because of the necessity for VEOs to have a modicum of modern education, most of them are young men from the south of the island, where schooling has been available for a longer period.

Each village elects a Village Development Committee (VDC) of twenty members. This body acts as a court, settling minor disputes and sending major ones on to the Divisional Executive Officer in Kirongwe (who acts as a lay magistrate) or the District Court in Kilindoni. It also discusses communications from the administration, and on occasion tries to interest the administration in the problems of the village; for example, during my stay in the village frequent concern about the poor water supply was expressed to the administration.

VDC meetings are also in theory TANU branch meetings, and are attended by the *majumbe*—the heads of the ten-house TANU cells—and the elected Village TANU secretary.[1] While I was staying in the village, an appointed and salaried TANU secretary was sent to live in the village by the TANU office in Kilindoni, and he too attended meetings. On average the VDC meets about once a week, but very few of these meetings are attended by all the members and *majumbe*. Normally the quorum consists of a few members and *majumbe*, and any interested passers-by, together with people who have disputes which they want discussed. Meetings convened in order to listen to visiting officials—TANU, administration, or technical personnel—generally have a larger attendance, as do meetings at which elections take place.

However, at the time of field-work, most decisions regarding administrative and political matters, and the settlement of disputes, were taken not by the VDC as a body, but rather by the small number of office-holders who wield effective political power in the village. These are the Chairman and Vice-Chairman of the VDC, the *Diwan* (District Council Representative), the VEO, and the two TANU secretaries (one elected by the villagers, the other sent in by the District TANU office). Let us examine each of these people in turn:

Principal office-holders

The Village Chairman, a Gunya, is the only male Sharif in the village. He has held his office for two terms, in fact since the post was instituted. On both occasions no contested election took place. One reason for this seems to be that, when new types of official posts are introduced into such a society, people tend on the whole to be either wary of becoming involved or else uninterested. Only as the extent of power attached to the posts becomes apparent and their permanence assured, do people become interested in holding office and elections begin to be contested.[2] It is thus not too difficult for people who are already in a position of some influence to achieve office; such people may be thought of as 'natural leaders' by the villagers, and in addition may themselves be astute enough to perceive the benefits of working within a new system and trying to turn it to their own advantage.

The Gunya Sharif, then, was seen by the villagers as suitable on several counts. He is literate in Roman as well as Arabic script, mainly because of his residence for long periods in Dar es Salaam. There he also acquired an air of sophistication which impresses the villagers. He came to power while he was still married to the daughter of the Imam, whom he has since divorced; he would thus have had the support of powerful affines. In spite of the fact that he never participates in religious activities, his religious and social status are of course unimpeachable in the eyes of the villagers.

However, the Chairman is frequently away for long periods (in 1966 he was often sick and visited hospitals in Kilindoni and Dar es Salaam), and even when he is in the village he does not always take the lead. His mother's brother, also a Gunya, acts as Chairman in the absence of his nephew. At one time, before the introduction of the present system, this man held the post of Village Headman. He is extremely learned in the Koran, and is usually referred to as Malim (*mwalim*), rather than by his own name, even though he does not teach. Meetings, particularly to discuss disputes, are often held at his house, rather than at the TANU office.

In what does the power of the Chairman and, in this case, the Vice-Chairman consist? First of all there is their role in settling disputes. The VDC, as already intimated, acts as a court, and can either reach a compromise settlement or else impose a punishment for wrongdoing. If the disputants do not agree to the verdict of the VDC, which often in effect means that of the Chairman and his uncle, then they can take the case to the Divisional Executive Officer in Kirongwe, and if he cannot settle it to the court in Kilindoni, but in most cases the DEO and magistrate tend to uphold the verdict of the VDC. In some instances the VDC will refuse permission to take the case any further, and if the disputants nevertheless go to Kirongwe or Kilindoni the officials will refuse to deal with it without a letter from the village Chairman.

Secondly, most official letters from the government are sent to the Chairman, and he is supposed to make their contents known to the VDC and to the village as a whole. Conversely, he has easier access to authority than the average villager, and a word from the Chairman to the administration counts for far more than one from anyone else in the village. Thus, for example, when one of the shopkeepers was discovered to be selling a low quality flour for the price of high quality flour, a letter from the Chairman to the authorities placed the shop-keeper in danger of losing his licence. The Chairman in fact decides whether or not such a complaint should be made to Kilindoni, or merely settled within the village. Similarly, when another man wished to set up a shop, he had to have a letter of recommendation from the Chairman before he could obtain a licence. The point is that most villagers have to deal with the government through the Chairman, and he can decide how to handle the matter, and whether to pass it on to the appropriate officials in Kilindoni or not.

Apart from the benefits of his role as intermediary between government and villagers the Chairman, along with other officials, is able to obtain loans either from the District Council or from the Co-operative Society. When these loans were first instituted, they were made available only to those thought to be reliable, and this meant either people who were fairly wealthy or else those holding official posts. In 1966, the Chairman obtained a loan, and bought a *wando* fishing trap, with which he made a lot of money.

Why is it that these men in particular (the Chairman and his uncle) are able to command so much power in the village? One important factor is their high socio-religious status. This is recognized by everyone in the village, including such people as the Sheikh and the Imam, with whom they have affinal relations (cf. Case 18). The Gunya do, in most contexts, interact with the high status members of descent group A; this is symbolized publicly by the fact that Gunya women cook at feasts with descent group A women.

On the other hand the Gunya can, when it suits them, stress their lack of strong kin affiliations in the village. They are not after all members of any of the six descent groups, nor are they caught up in the disputes between the *tarika* societies, nor do they seek office in the mosque, nor do they practise spirit possession. In other words, in every context in which the village is divided, usually along descent group lines, they stand apart, and stress that they are 'strangers' and 'neutral'. As such, it can be argued that they are peculiarly suited to settling disputes. In short, they are in a position to have their cake and eat it; they can rank themselves with the highest socio-religious stratum, and gain respect from the villagers, and support from other people of high status, and yet, when necessary, they can claim that they are divorced from all that makes for contention and strife in the village.

Another elected official who is of importance is the Diwan, the village representative on the Mafia District Council. This post also carries a certain amount of power, although rather different from that of the Chairman. The District Council meets monthly in Kilindoni, and discusses such matters as roads, schools, and dispensaries. Obviously each councillor is expected to press for money to be spent on improvements in his own village. The councillor takes requests from the villagers, such as for a well to be dug, or traps for wild animals to be supplied.

The post carries various 'perks'. One is that the Diwan is able to travel to Kilindoni monthly at the expense of the Council. He is thus in frequent contact with the centre of political manoeuvres in the Island. He can become a 'big man' not just in the village, but also in the District arena. Some men holding this post have even been to conferences in Dar es Salaam. A second advantage is that the Diwan, like the Chairman, is one of the first in line for any loans that might be available. With a loan from the District Council in 1965, the Minazini Diwan bought a large fishing net.

The Minazini Diwan, re-elected for a third term at the end of 1966 (cf. Case 15 below), is the son of the Imam, and is married to the Sheikh's sister (cf. Fig. 13). He is also deputy Imam of the Friday mosque. As a member of the A descent group, and in particular as a pious and learned man, and one closely connected with the Sheikh, he is of the highest socio-religious status.

Before the present Diwan was elected, the post was held by his cousin, who is also a member of the A descent group, and is a mosque official and *halifa* of the Minazini Sheikh's *tarika* society (cf. Fig. 13). During the latter's Diwanship, he was chosen by the District Council to become a Village Executive Officer, and sent to work in Kirongwe

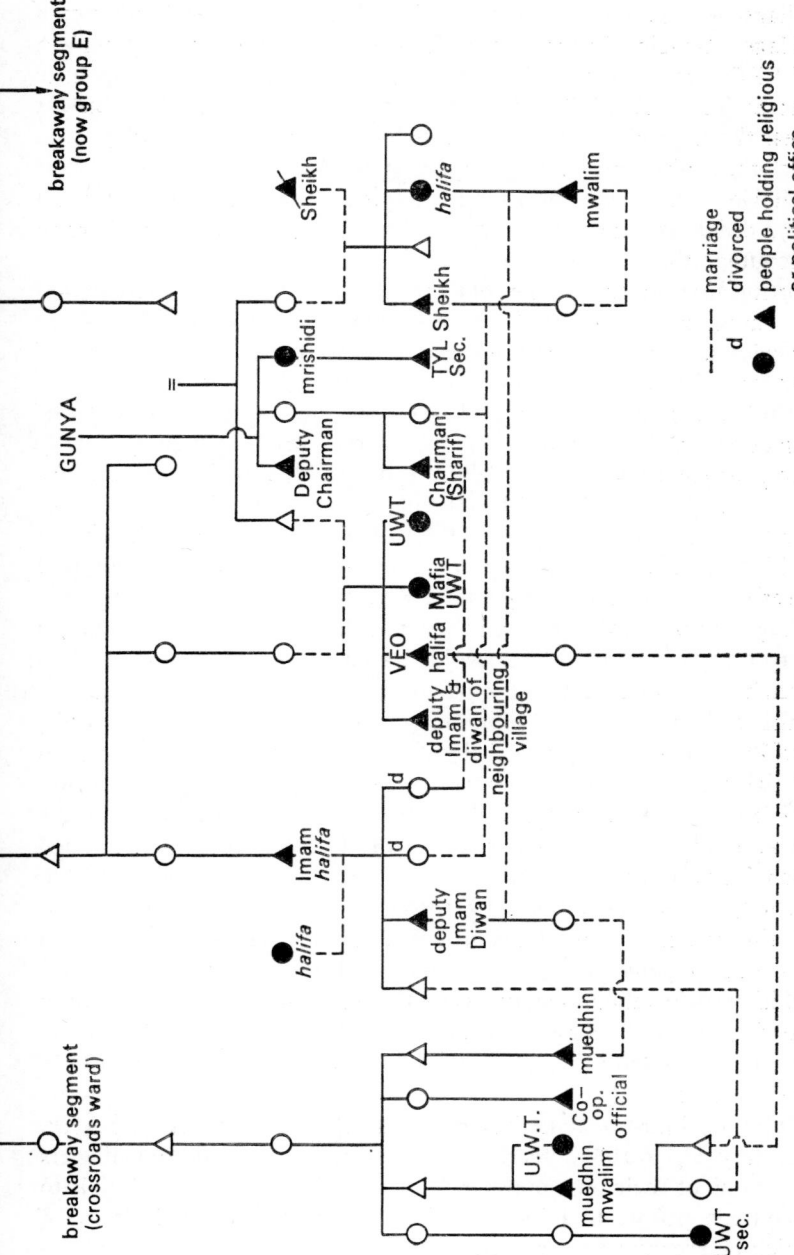

FIG. 13 *Section of Descent Group A showing religious and political office-holders and some marriages*

village. In mid-1966, he was transferred to work as VEO in his own village, Minazini. Prior to his appointment there had been a succession of VEOs from the south of the Island, and most of them had little success in Minazini. The villagers resented their dress (they did not wear the traditional and respectable long white gown, *kanzu*, or even a cloth, *shuka*, but rather western-style trousers and shirts), their behaviour (they did not attend mosque or pray, and some of them even drank), their youth, and the things that the VEOs were there to encourage them to do, namely, as already stated, tax-collecting, reporting any serious breaches of the peace, or crimes, such as theft, and encouraging the self-help schemes. The VEO was responsible for drawing up a rota for the ten house units so that each day the men of two units turned out to work on the teacher's house.

In the latter part of 1965, and early 1966, people grew tired of turning up at meetings at which they were harangued by the current VEO about attendance of their children at school, growing cotton, and co-operating on the self-help scheme. However, when, in mid-1966, the Minazini man who had been the VEO in Kirongwe was transferred to his own village, things went much more smoothly. He did not hold meetings to tell people what to do. Because he knew everyone in the village, he was able to go and see people as needed; there was no longer any possibility of tax avoidance or 'hiding' children. In addition, he had much more success with the self-help scheme, which was finished the same year. Undoubtedly he understood Minazini people, and knew how to behave. Furthermore, he was respected as a person of high socio-religious status; he is a member of descent group A, and *halifa* of the Minazini Sheikh's *tarika*, and a Deputy Imam of the mosque. He also had the support of his kin, who thereby condoned such innovations as the setting up of a women's organization (cf. Case 17 below). To a more limited but nonetheless significant extent, he also had the support and approval of the villagers who expected someone like him to be in a position of authority. His qualifications, i.e. high socio-religious status, were the ones which in their eyes fitted him for office; of course he had other qualifications too: literacy, and a strong personality, which had led to his being chosen as a VEO in the first place.

The third post of some importance in the village is that of TANU secretary. Up to 1966, this was a purely elective post, and the villagers chose one of their own number. The main job of the Secretary is to encourage people to join TANU and pay their subscriptions, of which he receives 10 per cent.

The man who holds this post provides an interesting example of social mobility. His parents were freed slaves, who had however amassed some wealth, as a result of his father being 'adopted' by a woman from descent group E as her 'brother' (this seems to have been a not uncommon occurrence). She helped him to acquire a good Koranic education, and he became a teacher, which gave him some religious status. Both of the sons and the daughter of this ex-slave are extremely religious and the men attend mosque regularly. Both are also successful traders to Dar es Salaam and Zanzibar. Despite their low social status they have been able to improve their position through religiosity and wealth to the point where both brothers are married to 'free born' women (the only men of slave descent in the village to do so), and one of them holds an official post in the village. However, their ability to rise in the social hierarchy is of course limited by their birth. Thus they are married to women of fairly low socio-religious status, and the post of TANU secretary is not as important as that of Chairman or Diwan.

In 1966 salaried government-appointed TANU secretaries were sent to all villages. Their job was to 'bring TANU to the people' in a more forceful way than the village secretaries had done before. Most of them were youths from the south of Mafia, and therefore greeted with as much suspicion as the previous VEOs had been. As this system only began at the end of my stay, I was unable to see what sort of a role the new TANU secretary plays in village politics; however, I later heard that the Minazini TANU secretary married a village girl, a member of descent groups B and F.

The final post of any importance in the village is that of the Co-operative official. This man is chosen by members of the Co-operative society as a whole, only some of whom are Minazini villagers. The Co-operative officials receive the copra at the market, and weigh it and pay the farmers. They are in a position, therefore, to reject copra which they consider is unripe or 'dirty'. In addition, since loans were by 1966 being channelled through the Co-operative society, they have a voice in deciding how loans are to be allocated. In theory, only those who are members of the society are eligible to receive loans, but many people who do not even own coconut trees, much less belong to the Co-operative, also try to get loans.

It is obvious that the Co-operative official potentially has an enormous amount of power, since he can reject or agree to buy copra which, as already pointed out in Chapter 1, is the main source of cash income for the majority of villagers; furthermore, the Co-operative is

also the channel through which loans are requested and granted, and such loans are virtually the only means of improving a villager's economic position.

The man who fills this post is a somewhat different type of person from the officials already discussed, and two reasons may account for this. First of all, he is not elected by the villagers but by members of the Co-operative as a whole, only some of whom are Minazini villagers. Secondly, the Co-operatives on Mafia were very new institutions indeed at the time of field-work. They were only set up towards the end of 1964; prior to that date, Indian traders in Kilindoni bought up all the Island's copra, and exported it to Dar es Salaam. The whole concept of a co-operative society was at that time so novel, that it is perhaps not surprising that somewhat different qualities were looked for in the Co-operative officials, than in those who filled such posts as Chairman and Diwan in the village.

The Co-operative official is not a man of very high status, since, although he is a member of descent group A, he is also a member of group F. Furthermore, he has not chosen, like some people of similar mixed descent, to stress only his links with people of high status—he does not live in an A group ward, nor does he participate in any of the activities of A group members, such as attending mosque, or belonging to the Minazini Sheikh's *tarika*. He is in fact what may be described as a 'new' type of man. He is quite young, only about 30 years of age, whereas the other officials tend to be in their forties. He is relatively wealthy as a result of his trading activities. He is highly intelligent, and has taught himself to read and write in Roman script.

To what extent does his success as a 'big man' in the Co-operative and his wealth as a trader affect his position in the village? In 1965 he divorced his wife, a member of descent group B, for adultery, and then asked the Minazini Sheikh for permission to marry his daughter, a girl who had just reached puberty. The Sheikh refused. The following year this man built the finest house in the village, and his power became greater because of the increasing difficulty the villagers had in marketing their copra, and because loans were now channelled through the Co-operative society. The Co-operative official told me privately that the Sheikh now wished him to marry his daughter, but that he had himself refused, because he was by then engaged to a young girl in a neighbouring village, and arrangements for the marriage were well advanced. Unfortunately, there was no way of checking whether or not the Sheikh would have married his daughter to this man, but if the claims were true then it might be said that he had translated his political and economic status into social status, and without using the traditional method of religiosity.

Previously, by stressing his membership of group A, and affiliating with that group in most contexts, this man could have had fairly high status. But he had used new criteria to improve his position in the hierarchy. It seems that such criteria are likely to become increasingly important as less emphasis is placed on religiosity as an essential criterion for high status, and therefore for political office.

Factors in political power

What do all these office holders have in common? First of all may be distinguished their high socio-religious status. The Chairman is a Sharif, the Deputy Chairman a Gunya and a *mwalim*; the Diwan is the son of the Imam, married to the Sheikh's sister, and he himself is the Deputy Imam and an official of the Sheikh's *tarika*. Similarly, the VEO is a member of descent group A, closely related to the Sheikh and the Imam, and he holds mosque and *tarika* posts. Even the Co-operative official is a member of descent group A (cf. Fig. 13). The only office holder of low social status is the TANU secretary, but he is at least highly religious.

Secondly, most of the above are reasonably sophisticated, by village standards. The Chairman and Deputy have spent long periods living in Dar es Salaam, and visit the capital frequently, as does the Co-operative official. The Diwan and VEO have both visited Zanzibar, where they have relatives, and the TANU secretary makes regular trading trips there. Furthermore, most of these men have made an effort to acquire literacy in Roman script (of course, they have all received a Koranic education, and are therefore already literate in Arabic script). As far as I know, only one or two other adult villagers are to any degree literate in Roman script.

Thirdly, most of them are reasonably wealthy men. All of them are heads of 'surplus' households (cf. Chapter 1), and the only one of their number who was not already in this category prior to obtaining office is the Chairman, who has made most of his money during office. The Diwan and the VEO own large numbers of coconut trees, and the Deputy Chairman and the TANU secretary are both highly successful traders; the latter is also a semi-skilled carpenter. On the whole, people of high socio-religious status are in the top economic bracket in Minazini; this applies particularly to those who hold political or religious offices. It is much easier for a man who is well-to-do to achieve office than it is for a man who can hardly make ends meet. For one thing, people in the former category do not need to work quite so hard in the fields, since they have the necessary cash to buy food, and so have extra time to give to political and religious matters.

It must be emphasized however that lack of money is not necessarily a bar to achieving office; the Village Chairman is a prime example of this, although of course in his case his poverty prior to election was mitigated by his high status as a Gunya and particularly as a Sharif. The main factor is socio-religious status, rather than economic status; there are after all many men in the village who are reasonably wealthy by local standards, but who would never achieve religious, or until very recently, political office.

Political change

The fact that a 'self-made' man, whose socio-religious status is fairly modest, can rise to a position of importance in the Co-operative is undoubtedly a sign of change. Another was the near defeat in the 1966 election of the incumbent Diwan:

CASE 15
The election for the Diwanship, 1966

The 1966 election for the diwanship was contested by the incumbent whom I shall call X who has already been shown to be a man of high socio-religious status—deputy Imam of the mosque and brother-in-law of the Sheikh—and a man of low socio-religious status, to whom I shall refer as Y, a member of descent groups E and F, and a member of a land spirit possession guild. The latter is also a relatively poor man.

Each contestant had to send a list of 25 supporters to the District Council Office in Kilindoni prior to being accepted as candidate. Y's supporters were almost all fellow descent group F members, two others were of slave descent, one, rather surprisingly was a Gunya, and the remaining two were descent group E members. I was unable to obtain the list of supporters for the incumbent X, but they would almost certainly have been members of descent group A, and perhaps of descent group B as well.

At the time of this election, it was plain that many people in the village, perhaps for the first time, were beginning to question the fact that people of high socio-religious status held office almost as a matter of right. There was voiced a certain resentment against 'those who wear *kanzu* (i.e. long white gowns, worn by the men for feasts or attending mosques, but never for manual work of any kind), and spend their time praying and politicking, and not working as hard as we do', etc. It seems likely that the new ideals of egalitarianism, heard frequently on the radio (there were three in the village, two owned by shopkeepers) and from visiting government officials, were beginning to take root in the minds of the villagers.

However, another factor in the election was the fact that the Pokomo man was very much disliked on personal grounds throughout the village, and his name was a by-word for gossip, slander, and exaggeration. Had this not been the case, it is likely that a candidate standing against the incumbent might well have won, if for no other reason than the fact that many people obviously wished to protest against the hegemony of the descent group A people. As it was, the incumbent Diwan won a very narrow victory (the voting figures were 103 to 94) and was returned to office.

A very similar process was discernible in a neighbouring village during the same elections:

CASE 16
The Diwan in a neighbouring village loses the 1966 election

The Diwan in this village is in fact a member of descent group A, and closely related to the Diwan in Minazini (cf. Fig. 14). Prior to holding the position of Diwan he had been Chairman of the village. He had been among the earliest people in Mafia to join TANU, and he was widely known as a successful politician on a district as well as village level. He is also a learned and religious man.

The campaign against him in his village was apparently conducted by people who said that they resented his continual air of 'superiority'. In the election, he was overwhelmingly defeated by 155 to 78 votes.

The fact remains however that, on the whole, the people who have traditionally held positions of authority are still in many instances best placed to do so. A good example of this is provided by another election which occurred, while I was in the field, for village committees and a District Chairman of the Tanzania Women's Union (*Ummoja wa Wanawake wa Tanzania*):

CASE 17
The election of the District Chairwoman of the UWT

The UWT had for some time been active in the south of the island, organizing women's literacy classes and trying to take women more politically aware. The Chairwoman was the sister of the Diwan mentioned in the previous case, who had been encouraged to take up a political career after the breakdown of her marriage.

Elections for a new Chairwoman and Committee at the district level were held in 1966. Previously the post of Chairwoman had not been contested, but on this occasion an opposing faction had arisen in the south of the Island, and put up another candidate.

It was no coincidence then that only a few days before the election, when it was being widely surmised throughout the Island that the incumbent Chairwoman would lose, she came to Minazini and the other northern villages, and set up UWT branches in each of them, with a village chairwoman, deputy, and secretary. In Minazini, she informed the VEO (who is her half-brother, cf. Fig. 14) and the Diwan (also a classificatory brother) of her coming, and asked them to gather the women together. Not surprisingly it was mainly members of group A who attended the meeting, and who elected officials from among themselves. In fact, the deputy chairwoman in Minazini is the sister of the Mafia chairwoman.

A few days later, the three Minazini committee members went off to Kilindoni to vote in the UWT election. The incumbent Chairwoman was returned to office. It is likely that she also had the support of most of the delegates from the newly constituted northern village branches of the UWT who would probably vote for her rather than for a woman from southern Mafia who would be unknown to them.

Thus although there appears to be some change,[3] on the whole people of high socio-religious status are still in an extremely strong position and seem likely to continue to control most of the political offices, at least for a while. For one thing, the value placed on orthodox Islam has not changed, even though other criteria for office may be becoming more important. But even so the people who traditionally held office have seized new opportunities; a few have made themselves literate in Roman script, and most have ensured that their children should be so by sending them to school (it is interesting to note that the only four girls in school beyond the age of puberty in 1966 were the daughters of the Sheikh, the Arab, the Diwan, and the VEO). Furthermore, these people have always been among the wealthier members of the community, and those who have held office under the new system have been first in line for loans. Traditionally, people of high socio-religious status had wider horizons and more contacts with Dar es Salaam and Zanzibar than others, and this gave them a greater sophistication. They were able to use their kin links very efficiently when necessary, partly because they were all literate, and so could send letters. They have been quick to see the advantage of aligning themselves with the nationalist movement and TANU, and of not opposing innovations, at least not publicly, but rather condoning them where they can do so without incurring too much opprobrium from the villagers. Thus for example, they have supported government schooling for all children, but when attempts were made by the government to set up a cotton-growing co-operative, a move which infuriated most of the villagers, most of the village officials and their close supporters took care to remain neutral.

In sum, the villagers still tend to see such people as being particularly suitable to hold office, largely because of their traditional status, while the latters' acceptance of new ideals, at least in public, causes them to find favour with government officials.

Marriage strategies

In concluding this chapter, I want to return to the subject of marriage, and to discuss the way in which it is used as a strategy in obtaining or maintaining socio-religious status and hence positions of power in the community.

On the whole, people of high socio-religious status, and in particular those wielding power (either through a political or a religious post), tend to practise discriminatory marriage policies. They usually marry only among themselves, or else with people of similar status living outside Minazini village.

To a limited extent marriage may be termed hypergamous; it is somewhat more acceptable for a man of high status to marry a woman of low status than vice versa. (There are several people of high socio-religious status in the village whose mothers were actually slaves, but who took their status from their father.) Thus the success of a man in marrying a woman of higher status than himself usually means that he is recognized as having improved his own status in some way. This is what the TANU secretary had succeeded in doing, and what the Co-operative official was trying to do.

On the other hand, however, because the hierarchical system co-exists with a system of cognatic descent, in which descent through the mother is extremely important, it is highly unlikely that a man of very high status would marry a woman of low status, and particularly unlikely that a man from a family noted for religiosity would marry a woman from a family deeply involved in spirit possession. As the Sheikh's sister put it, 'It is impossible for us to send our young people just anywhere to get married. Other people are not as particular as we are about purity (*usafi*) and other such matters, and their standard of living is lower.' By 'purity' she could have been referring to hygiene, purity of descent, ritual purity, or a combination of these, while 'standard of living' was a reference not only to material things, but also to a religious way of life.

A good example of the way people of the highest status tend to marry is provided by the family of the Imam, who has nine children, five sons and four daughters. One of his sons (the *Diwan*) is married to the sister of the Sheikh, another to the daughter of the *muedhin* of the mosque, who is also a *mwalim* (he is a member of the breakaway segment of descent group A); the other three sons are all married to women who are fellow descent group A members. Strategic marriages were likewise made for his daughters. The eldest married the son of the old Sheikh, and when he died she married his brother, the present Sheikh; the second daughter was married to the Sharif who was at the time of field-work the Chairman of the VDC; the third is married to a man who was until recently the Chairman of a neighbouring village; the fourth is married to her cousin, and fellow member of group A. (Some of the marriages are shown in Fig. 14.)

Marriage choices, then, can be viewed in a number of ways; firstly, the ideal of marriage to a member of one's personal network (*jamaa*), secondly, marriage to a fellow descent group member—both of these have already been discussed in Chapter 2—and thirdly, marriage to a person of more or less equivalent socio-religious status. In the case of people at the top and bottom of the hierarchy in the village, statistical patterns often realize all three ideals.

However, it must not be forgotten that the situation is not a simple one, that the three models do not always neatly fit together; indeed, it is the very fact that they do not which makes for a dynamic hierarchy, as is shown in the following case history:

CASE 18

The dispute between the Imam and the Sheikh

The husband of the only female Sharif in the village (i.e. the sister of the Chairman) died. The Imam wished his son, the Diwan (already married to the sister of the Sheikh), to marry the widow. However she was eventually taken as a third wife by the Sheikh, who was already married to the Imam's daughter, as well as to the sister of a wealthy Gunya, who was the Diwan of a village in central Mafia. The Imam was extremely angry, and caused trouble between the Sheikh and his first wife, who was the Imam's daughter. Finally she left her husband and he divorced her.

It appears that she was not on very good terms with her father because of this, and she did not go to live in his cluster, as is usual in the case of divorced women, but lived on her meadow land. Later she decided to marry a man from a neighbouring village who was a Pokomo.

At this time the Imam was in Zanzibar, so the suitor turned to her classificatory father's brother and asked his opinion. He agreed to the marriage, and undertook all the arrangements.

Her brother, the Diwan, did not hear of the matter until the arrangements were quite far advanced and the suitor had already made over some of the marriage payments. The Diwan was utterly opposed to the marriage, and pointed out to his sister in the strongest terms that she, as the daughter of the Imam and ex-wife of the Sheikh, could not think of marrying a man of much lower status (he was in fact not only a Pokomo but also a cow-herd).

After some time, the Diwan persuaded his sister to agree to marry a man whom he knew in the south of the Island, a wealthy man and one renowned for his piety and learning.

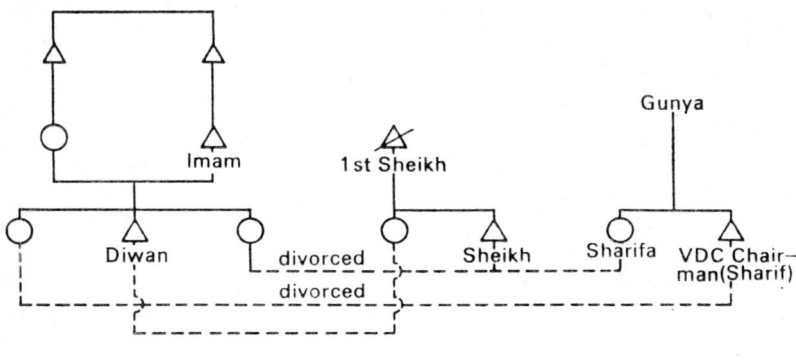

FIG. 14

Dispute between the Imam and the Sheikh

One aspect of this dispute concerns the re-marriage of the Sharif woman. The Imam wished his son to marry her, as that would have shown their equality with the Gunya Sharifs. He definitely did not wish the Sheikh to marry her, both because this might have shown the Sheikh's status to be higher than that of the Imam's family, and also because the position of his own daughter, the Sheikh's wife, would be threatened by a co-wife of such high status. The fact that the Sheikh succeeded, against the opposition of the Imam, in marrying this woman only confirmed his somewhat superior status.

Another aspect of the dispute relates to the re-marriage of the Imam's daughter, divorced by the Sheikh. Her brother realized that he and the whole family would 'lose face' by one of their women, even a woman who had already been married, marrying a man of such low social status. He therefore put pressure[4] on his sister to reject the man of her own choice and marry a man whom she had never seen, but who was of high social status. The husband chosen for her by her brother would also of course provide the latter with a contact in the south of the Island, which might prove politically useful.

A concern for social status leads to many marriages taking place with equals outside the village, as happened with the Imam's daughter in the marriage discussed in Case 18. There are numerous other examples in descent group A. The daughter of the VEO married a Kilindoni politician, and the Sheikh married the sister of the Gunya Diwan in another village; in turn, the latter also married the Sheikh's sister. The effect of such a large number of inter-village marriages is to reduce still further the number of other Minazini descent groups in which group A people can claim membership.

There are also people within group A who are not considered to be of such high status as those I have been discussing. Various reasons may be given why these people do not enjoy the same status as other members of group A. One is that they are not as closely connected to the families of the Sheikh and the Imam; this applies for instance to the Co-operative official. Another reason, which also applies to this man, is mixed Mbwera–Pokomo descent. A third reason is that it is not sufficient just to be born a member of descent group A; it is necessary to interact in a number of contexts with other members, and particularly, to participate in activities, such as mosque attendance, which confer status. Again, the Co-operative official did not live in an A group ward, nor did he cultivate A group land; more importantly for his status-rating, he did not attend mosque, nor the Minazini Sheikh's *tarika*.

Those members of group A who are considered of lower status than the close kin of the Sheikh and the Imam are thus likely to marry with Mbwera of other descent groups, although rarely with people of Pokomo descent. In spite of this, descent group A is the most highly intra-married group in the village; no fewer than 50 per cent of its men are, or have been, married to fellow members of the group.

One of the effects of the marriage policies of members of group A has been to reduce the number of people who are members of it, which has made it easier to conserve power in the hands of a few people. In addition many of the members owe all their loyalties to this group, since they have no membership of other descent groups. Some of the more astute members of group A perceive this, and take it into account when formulating marriage plans. They, more than others, tend to view marriages as taking place within the descent group, whereas others tend to see intra-descent group marriages primarily as taking place within the *jamaa* (cf. Chapter 2). Of course, the fact that group A is so small (with a total of only 77 adult members) means that in any case most members can trace their kin links with one another, whereas in other larger groups this is not always possible.

Since group A is not a completely endogamous unit, social mobility is possible. Non-members of the group are married because of their political or religious position and/or wealth, either within or outside the village. This leads to a dynamic hierarchy in which people use marriage as a strategy to consolidate or improve their social status. This competition for status goes on even within the descent group itself, while outside group A other people use this descent group as a reference point, and those who wish to raise, or demonstrate a rise in, their socio-religious status will attempt to marry into it.

Conclusion

This chapter has been about the relationship between political power and socio-religious status. As has frequently happened elsewhere, with the introduction of a new political system, it is usually those who already wield power who are best placed to take advantage of the new system. People of high socio-religious status are generally thought to be 'more fitted' to rule; they are the best-educated people, and usually have wide-ranging contacts outside the confines of the village. In Minazini, marriage for such people is also a political strategy, with intra-descent group marriage enabling power to be kept in fewer hands, and marriage with important people in other villages creating ties with a wider élite.

However the situation is not static; since independence there has been considerable emphasis placed by the government and TANU on egalitarianism and African socialism, which provides an alternative ideology to the older hierarchical ideals concerned with socio-religious status. A new category of people is beginning to seek, and in some cases, to gain political power. However, it seems likely that most such people will seek to translate their new status into the terms of the old, chiefly by means of marriage.

CHAPTER 8

CONCLUSION

In this book I have been discussing property and power relations which, in Minazini, are expressed in several frameworks or 'idioms' (Leach 1961)—the descent groups, the personal network, and the socio-religious hierarchy. Each of these constitutes a 'conscious' or actor's model (Levi-Strauss 1953) although, in fact, the actors do not always separate their overall view of their society into three distinct models.[1]

The first part of the book, Chapters 2 to 4, was concerned with property relations, that is the distribution of residential and cultivable land rights. Although nearly all land is seen as the property of the descent groups and their constituent segments, people often explain their choices about where to live and cultivate in terms of their *jamaa*, rather than their descent groups. For example, for residence decisions people may see themselves acting as members of a particular descent group by going to live in a ward associated with that group. But they also talk about residence in terms of ownership of coconut trees and the developmental cycle of clusters, which is complicated by the frequency of divorce and fostering; in short, they are making choices with reference to their *jamaa*. The same situation applies to land rights: most cultivable land is obtained through descent group membership, but people may also express this in terms of their kinship relations with an Elder or Guardian of a descent group.

In the second part of the book another framework, that of the socio-religious hierarchy, was introduced. Although this is derived from the East African coastal hierarchical system, in Minazini it is also associated with the descent groups. Members of descent group A, partly because of their connection with the Sheikh, have on the whole higher status than members of other descent groups; they attend mosque more often, control most of the mosque offices, and are members of the exclusive Minazini Sheikh's *tarika* society. Members of descent group F, on the other hand, have lower status than members of the other descent groups, because it is the members of this group who practise land spirit possession.

On the East African coast, as in other parts of the Muslim world, the ideology states that those of high socio-religious status are peculiarly fitted to rule, and in Minazini this has meant that there are more members of group A holding important political office (along with the high status Gunya) than members of other descent groups, and that until very recently no member of group F held any political position of importance.

Sometimes the conscious models complement each other; sometimes they are apparently in conflict. Thus, for example, the ideal of multiple membership of cognatic descent groups is complemented by the ideal of kin marriage within the *jamaa*. But the ideal of cognatic descent groups being basically of the same type, both structurally and functionally, is in conflict with the ideal of the socio-religious hierarchy. Such contradictions are not of course necessarily perceived by the actors themselves.

In seeking to understand and analyse a society, we need, of course, to take account of the conscious models, which may have a more or less useful explanatory value; in any case, whatever their degree of usefulness, they are, as Levi-Strauss has pointed out, part of the range of observed facts (ibid. 527). Thus in an attempt to formulate a mechanical model (by which I mean 'a set of jural rules' following Leach 1961) we must include all three conscious models already discussed. However if we try to relate the mechanical model to what people actually do, that is, to a statistical model,[2] we find that there is often a considerable gap between them. In other words, neither type of model provides a total explanation of the facts under consideration.

In the article by Levi-Strauss in which the distinction between the foregoing types of models was first made explicit, he pointed out that:

'The best model will always be that which is *true*, that is, the simplest possible model which, while being extracted exclusively from the facts under consideration, also makes it possible to account for all of them' (ibid.: 526).

However, as I have already stated, neither a mechanical model nor a statistical model provides a total explanation of all the facts. In the process of bridging the gap between these two types of models a third type, variously termed a 'self-interest model' (Scheffler 1965), an 'action model' (Ogan 1966) or a 'decision model' (Keesing 1967a) emerges. Keesing defines this kind of model as follows:

'We use "decision model" in a fairly broad sense to denote an ethnographic description that is actor-oriented and based on the categories of the culture under study, i.e. one that is "emic". Its minimal properties are that it (1) defines the situation or context in a culturally meaningful way; (2) defines the range of culturally acceptable courses of action in that situation; and provides either (3) a set of rules for making appropriate decisions under culturally possible combinations of circumstances . . . or (4) a set of strategies for deciding among alternatives.' (1967a:2).

The 'decision model' then, should explain a situation in a more fundamental way than either a mechanical or statistical model alone, or indeed, than both of them together can do. But it must obviously relate to both the mechanical and statistical models, and it certainly does not do away with the necessity for constructing the former types of model.

Keesing, in extolling the virtues of the decision model, concludes that statistical models are 'clumsy instruments for describing social relations' (ibid.: 95). Scheffler too, while not castigating statistical models to the same extent, finds them useful as 'only the first descriptive analytical step' (ibid.: 291). While agreeing with Scheffler that it is necessary early in the analysis to construct statistical models, I would not agree that they can thereafter be discarded. For it is my contention that a statistical model *tests* the validity of the decision model, and that if the former model is at variance with the latter, then the decision model is either incorrect or only partially correct.

In this final chapter, then, I want to construct a more elaborate statistical model, by collating the numerical data already given about the descent groups, and to compare this with the decision model already given in the course of this book.

In Minazini descent groups are associated with specific sets of resources—land, status, and power. Descent group A members dominate the Friday mosque and the Minazini Sheikh's *tarika* society, as well as the more significant political posts in the village. Descent group F, on the other hand, holds most of the bush land of the village; its members also monopolize one of the chief healing rituals through their relationship with land spirits. Members of descent group E control the southern Sheikh's *tarika*, one of the sea-spirit guilds is also located in its ward, and nearly all its officials are members of group E.

We might thus justifiably expect that, in a situation of multiple group membership, people would tend to maximize their advantages by affiliating with those of their groups which control important resources, and, particularly, to associate with a given group in the context of the resource which it controls. Thus it would be expected that descent groups A, E, and F would attract a higher proportion of members to affiliate with them than would the other three groups which do not control such important resources.[3] Table 29 gives the overall pattern of affiliation to descent groups in the contexts of cultivation, residence, Islamic religious activities, spirit possession, and marriage.

In the first context, that of residence, no descent group controls more resources than any other. However, we find that groups A, E, and F have a majority of their members affiliating for residence purposes, while only a minority of the members of other groups reside in their wards. In fact, as we shall see, residence is consistent with choice in other contexts; people tend to live in the wards of those groups which control important resources.

Descent group F controls more land than any other group, and it is thus not surprising to find that a very high proportion of its members have, over a period of time, utilized their rights in this group. However, given the fact that many people have a number of choices about where they can cultivate, and that there are economic and physical constraints which also influence their decisions, we might expect that most people would utilize most of their options at some time or other. This does appear to be the case, for all the groups, with the exception of C which holds very little land, have attracted most of their members to affiliate with them in the context of cultivation.

Turning to religious activities, we would expect that there would be an inverse correlation between high mosque attendance and land spirit possession activities, and this is indeed the case. Group A has 50 per cent of its members attending mosque, while only 10 per cent of those with group F membership do so. The same applies to *tarika* society membership; nearly all the members of group A belong to the society of the Minazini Sheikh, while the majority of members of groups E and F belong to that of the southern Sheikh. This can be explained by the fact that members of the former group control the Minazini branch of this society, while group F members are excluded from the Minazini Sheikh's *tarika*. The other three descent groups are more divided in their *tarika* affiliations.

We would also expect that those descent groups which attract a majority of members to affiliate with them in most contexts would also have the highest figures for intra-marriage. One reason for this is that those descent groups which practise a high rate of intra-marriage would have as members more people with single membership, and not multiple membership. Conversely, if marriage is viewed as a strategy, then we would expect those groups which control resources to practise intra-marriage in an effort to keep control of the resources. This is indeed the case, with highest intra-marriage figures for groups A

TABLE 29
Descent group affiliation compared* (males† only)

Context of affiliation	Descent group					
	A	B	C	D	E	F
residence in ward	61%	31%	36%	36%	55%	66%
cultivating with descent group‡	70%	58%	18%	70%	70%	82%
Friday mosque attendance	50%	16%	25%	26%	16%	10%
Tarika member:						
Southern Sheikh	20%	52%	53%	70%	95%	86%
Minazini Sheikh	80%	48%	47%	30%	5%	14%
membership of land spirit guild	3%	32%	7%	16%	20%	33%
intra-marriage§	50%	27%	25%	40%	41%	47%

Notes: * For the purposes of my argument here I am treating the six sets or contexts in which descent groups are significant as comparable, even though I am aware that they are not all of the same level, and that comparison between them must be limited.

† Males only are considered in this table because in several of these contexts women have little choice about affiliation, e.g. residence or mosque attendance.

‡ Cultivation covers a six-year period 1961–6.

§ Intra-marriage means that either a first or subsequent marriage was with a woman of the same descent group.

and F, Groups D and E are not far behind whereas Group B, which is in the process of splitting into two segments, and group C both probably have lower rates because of their relative paucity of resources.

In sum then, Table 29 shows that those descent groups whose members control important resources attract a higher proportion of their members to affiliate with them than groups which do not; in Firth's terms, the former type of groups are 'more corporate', the latter type less so (Firth 1959a: 215–16, 1963: 23).

Another way of looking at the degree of 'corporateness' of groups might be to consider whether it is the same people who affiliate with any given descent group in a number of contexts. In other words, is there a core of descent group members who tend to affiliate with a given group in most possible contexts, or do people tend to utilize their membership of all their groups in a variety of contexts? For example, people who are members of descent group A might affiliate with that group only in terms of religious activities, while they might prefer to cultivate with other groups. Table 30 compares the percentages of members affiliating in different numbers of contexts.

TABLE 30
Frequency of affiliation with a descent group

Descent group	Number of contexts of affiliation							No. of adult male members
	6	5	4	3	2	1	0	
A	0%	30%	22%	10%	6%	19%	13%	38 (100%)
B	0%	5%	5%	20%	16%	33%	20%	55 (100%)
C	0%	0%	11%	14%	25%	18%	32%	28 (100%)
D	0%	2%	14%	34%	26%	18%	6%	51 (100%)
E	0%	5%	23%	34%	20%	14%	2%	44 (100%)
F	11·5%	29%	29%	13%	10%	4·5%	2·5%	112 (100%)

It is clear that two groups have a majority of their members affiliating with them in a majority of contexts. Over half (52 per cent) of those who are members of group A, and an even greater proportion (58 per cent) of those with group F descent, affiliate in four or more of the six contexts considered. For the other descent groups, the figures are much lower—28 per cent for group E, 16 per cent for group D, 11 per cent for group C, and 10 per cent for group B.

If we take only three or more contexts, we again find that group F remains the most 'corporate', with 82·5 per cent of members affiliating in three or more contexts, while groups A and E follow with 62 per cent and D with 50 per cent; groups B and C are far behind with only 30 per cent and 25 per cent respectively.

However, an important fact revealed by this table is that only one group has any members who affiliate only with that group in all possible contexts, and that is group F. This group has a high degree of intra-marriage, and in land it controls a major economic resource. But for most of the other groups, there are resources which are not held by them which people need, and for which they are forced to turn to other groups. Thus for example, many group A members obtain land from other descent groups, either through their membership of these groups or else through *jamaa* links.

On the whole, then, those groups which are most 'corporate' in terms of the resources which they control also tend to be most corporate in other contexts too. It would thus seem that some people find it advantageous to affiliate with only one descent group in most possible contexts. My observations indicate that it is the leaders of the institutions such as spirit possession guilds and *tarika* societies who fall into this category. Such people generally reside in the wards where these institutions are located, and this factor helps to explain why residence figures are consistent with figures in other contexts (cf. Table 29). This does not of course mean that residence can in any way be described as a 'closing factor' in descent group membership. There are many people who reside with one descent group, but interact in most other contexts with another group. A good example of this is provided by the man in Case 13 in Chapter 6, who lives in an F group ward, but in most other contexts affiliates with group B.

But people who find it most advantageous to utilize their multiple membership in this way are not usually leaders of activities, and indeed leadership is most often exercised by those who have only single descent group membership, because control of resources goes along with a very high degree of intra-marriage, and hence a reduction in the likelihood of multiple membership.

Groups which do not control important resources will not attract members to affiliate with them. Group C, for instance, has so little to offer its members that it is possible that many people do not bother to acknowledge their membership of it, and in time links have been forgotten. And here it is perhaps in order to note that obviously this is a system which changes over time; some groups have obviously come to prominence since the arrival of the Zanzibar Sheikh and the *tarika* societies, while others have declined in importance. Obviously if a descent group, or rather the members of a particular group, acquire control of a new resource, then people are anxious to activate their membership of that group, or else to marry into it, in order to ensure that their children have access to the resource.

We have then, in Minazini, an ideal system of unrestricted cognatic descent groups which are non-endogamous, and which have multiple functions. But in fact we find that the descent groups are not of the same order at all, and people do not affiliate with them in a random sort of way. In seeking to explain the differences between the mechanical and statistical models, it has been necessary to construct a third type of model which takes into account other conscious models and the way in which they relate to the descent group system, and also other factors which constrain choice. This third type of model—the decision model—can be tested by comparing it with the mechanical and statistical models, which is what I have tried to do in this chapter. I hope that, if it has done nothing else, it will have shown that 'the three different models in combination have more heuristic value than any of them alone' (Ogan ibid.: 190).

NOTES

Preface

1. Minazini, meaning 'among the coconut palms' is a fictitious name, as are the names of villagers.

Chapter 1

1. cf. Baumann 1896, King 1917, Revington 1936, Piggott 1941, Oliver and Mathew 1963.

2. Chittick 1957 et seq., 1961, Freeman-Grenville 1962.

3. Strictly speaking, the correct form is Wambwera (plural prefix *wa-*). However, in order to avoid confusing the reader not familiar with Bantu languages, I have retained only the singular form of this and other appellations, e.g. Pokomo, Gunya, throughout the book.

4. Mafia District Book.

5. Umbwera is the name of a place on the mainland.

6. In the 1967 census only 34 household heads gave their ethnic origin as 'Arab'. Assuming that the average household size of 3·4 persons revealed by this census also includes such people, this would give a total number of 'Arabs' on the Island as around 130. Such an enormous drop in numbers from the 663 persons of the 1957 census is probably explained by such people now preferring to categorize themselves as 'Africans'.

7. A Tanzanian (East African) shilling was in 1966 equivalent to a British shilling; it is divided into 100 cents; pounds are not used in East Africa.

8. The 1967 census showed that only 38 students from Mafia were attending secondary schools, while 1,787 were attending primary schools.

9. TANU is the Tanganyika African National Union, the only political party in mainland Tanzania.

10. Sharifs are descendants of the Prophet Mohammed. As such, they are of high religious status, and entitled to great respect (cf. Chapters 5 and 7, and Caplan 1974).

11. Although ex-slaves or their descendants are on the whole reluctant to admit their status, it was possible for me to obtain precise figures after I had been resident in the village for some time. Other informants were willing, in private, to categorize people as slaves, and of course such people did not appear in the genealogies of the descent groups as did the 'free born' Mbwera and Pokomo.

12. There is a government school between Minazini and a neighbouring village which caters for the children of both villages. It is a primary school, which in 1967 taught up to standard 6. The majority of boys over the age of seven attend, as do a few girls who are below the age of puberty.

13. Both copra and cashew nuts are marketed through the two local co-operatives in Kirongwe and Kilindoni. These are government-sponsored, and were initiated in 1964. Prior to that date, all copra and cashew nuts were bought up by the local

Indian traders. The co-operatives have run into various difficulties which have tended to make them unpopular. First of all, their establishment coincided with a slump in world copra prices and demand. This meant not only that the prices fell locally, but also that the copra which was accepted by the co-operatives had to be of a high quality. Much unripe or 'dirty' (i.e. smoke-dried, not sun-dried) copra had to be rejected. A second difficulty at the time of field-work was that the co-operatives tended to run out of cash with which to pay the farmers, particularly if flights from Dar es Salaam to the Island were delayed. This meant that the farmers were left with copra on their hands, and because of shrinkage its worth decreased with storage.

14. Expenses include wages of fellers and preparers of copra, and transportation of copra to Kirongwe market by donkey.

15. Even in a poor year expenses remain high, e.g. fellers are paid per tree, and not according to the number of nuts they fell.

16. It should be emphasized that these figures are only approximate and are given mainly with the intention of showing the disparity in the incomes of the male population.

Total incomes per annum were reckoned as follows:

coconut tree	2*s*. per tree
cattle	100*s*. per head
fishing	250*s*.
donkey	250*s*.
sailor	400*s*.
casual labourer	100*s*.
trader	500*s*.
herdsman	100*s*.
shaman	250*s*.–500*s*.
Koranic teacher	250*s*.–500*s*.
tailor	100*s*.–200*s*.

In fact, a few people made much more by being highly successful traders or shamans.

Chapter 2

1. In this respect, the descent groups in Minazini differ from some of those in Polynesia, where membership is often conferred by birth *and* residence, e.g. the *Kainga* of the Gilbert Islanders, as described by Goodenough (1955), and, to a lesser extent, the New Zealand Maori (Firth 1957, 1963).

2. Genealogies were obtained from older men and women, especially the Elders of descent groups, and were checked against personal genealogies given by a number of people. It does not seem very likely that the genealogies are 'telescoped', although they are certainly manipulated on occasion (e.g. cf. Chapter 4, Case 5).

3. In order to avoid confusing the reader with yet more local names, and also to reinforce the anonymity of the villagers, I have used letters to denote the descent groups. However, I should emphasize that these are in fact *named* groups.

4. It must be emphasized that the same Swahili terms do *not* necessarily have the same meaning on all parts of the coast. In this respect, a 'common' language makes the situation more, and not less complex (cf. Tanner 1959, Wijeyewardene 1961, Middleton 1961, Prins 1961, Lienhardt 1968 for the way in which these terms are used in various parts of the East African coast). Bailey 1965: 130–8 gives a summary of the literature on coastal kinship terms.

5. I am aware that all my figures regarding marriages and divorce are extremely

crude, since they take no account of age or duration of marriages. As has frequently been pointed out, it is extremely difficult to obtain precise figures for the incidence of divorce, and to discover whether it is increasing or decreasing in a society where most people have little idea of their ages, much less of the length of time they have been married.

6. Tanner (1959) and Wijeyewardene (1961), working on the mainland coast, both found cousin marriage to be more stable than non-cousin marriage.

7. The turban is associated with Arab dress, and as such is a sign of prestige on the coast.

8. The *mkaja* is a belt worn by women after child-birth.

Chapter 3

1. These constitute the only methods of acquiring trees; there is no mortgaging.

2. It is only under Shafei law that a *wakf* may be made in favour of descendants (cf. Anderson 1959). Other schools state that it must be left to a religious charity like a mosque. Most *wakf* property in Minazini is left to descendants, but one of the mosques is maintained by a *wakf* bequest.

3. This system of fostering (*ulezi*) is found throughout the coast. Tanner found that 37 per cent of children in villages around Pangani were fostered out (1959).

4. Joking relations (*utani*) exist between cross-cousins, and between grand-parents and grandchildren. In addition, there are joking relations of the same kind between 'tribes', e.g. between Pokomo and Gunya. At rites of passage, 'compensation' (*ugongo*) is paid to everyone with whom one has a joking relationship; similarly, joking relations can be called upon to perform certain tasks, such as digging the grave at a funeral.

The 'tribal' joking relationship is not of much significance in Minazini, but in the southern villages, where there is a far higher proportion of ex-slaves, and immigrants from the mainland, it is an important part of every rite of passage. At the same time, of course, it serves to demarcate the 'free born' from the slaves, since most joking relationships are between people of high status and low status, as in the case of the Pokomo and Gunya.

Chapter 4

1. Land tenure in Minazini village has many similarities with land tenure in Zanzibar Island among the Hadimu (cf. MacGeagh and Addis 1945, Pakenham 1947, Middleton 1961).

2. In translating *dawe* by 'meadow' I am following the Oxford Dictionary, which defines a meadow as 'a grass field, near to water'.

3. In fact, strictly speaking, freehold did not exist under either German or British rule, although during the latter period the courts tended to treat individual title acquired by 30 years occupancy as analogous to freehold (cf. Bailey 1965: 113–15).

4. It should be noted that my use of these terms does not correspond to the way in which they have been used by Gluckman (1943) and others. However, Minazini people themselves do make a distinction between various types of holder—a person who has obtained rights other than through being a primary holder will say '*nimebenda*' or '*nimeuga*' meaning 'I asked permission'.

5. It may have been no mere coincidence that the same man took both of Athman's fields; it is possible that there was some other dispute between them, and that Seleman was deliberately trying to annoy Athman. Unfortunately it was not possible to obtain any more details. The main point is that Seleman used government law to win his case.

6. In some contexts descent groups E and F tend to interact (cf. discussion of

tarika societies in Chapter 5). This may be because when group E was formed by people hiving off from group A, some of them married group F members. People often implied that there was a close relationship between members of group E and F, although no one seemed to know why this piece of meadow land was held by the two groups.

7. In other parts of Mafia many cases turn on this particular point. In Baleni village (where I spent 3 months), there are many cashew nut trees, and frequent disputes about their ownership. This is because until recently they were of no value, and in fact were planted by birds dropping the fruit seeds. With the sudden rise in the price of cashew nuts, and the drop in copra prices, cashew nut trees have become a considerable asset. Thus where two men have documents stating the boundaries of their coconut fields, and in between is a stretch of land which has come to contain cashew nut trees, both men may claim the latter trees.

Chapter 5

1. The *Maulid ya Barazanji* is a poem celebrating the birth of Mohammed, and telling of the wonders that occurred at the time. There are three versions—the full Arabic version by Ja'far bin Hassan al Abidin al-Barzanji al Madina, who lived from 1690–1766, an abridged version made by his grandson, and a Swahili version by the poet Sayid Mansab. In Mafia one of the Arabic versions is most commonly in use (cf. Harries 1962: 102 et seq.).

2. At the *Maulid* reading (*pilao*) rice and meat cooked together is served. But after the encirclement and blessing of the village (*kuzingua mji*) only meat is cooked. I have no explanation for this, but it may be connected with the fact that all the other northern villages are invited to the *Maulid* as guests, whereas the blessing of the village concerns only Minazini people, quite a number of whom take their meat home to consume it there.

3. The reason why I have considered only the male population in this table is that in the Conclusion I want to compare the various contexts of affiliation to descent groups, and women are not significant in all contexts, e.g. residence choices. However, the proportions would not be any different if I had included women as well as men in this table.

Chapter 6

1. I do not intend here to pursue fully the subject of spirit possession *per se*. This will be dealt with in a later publication.

2. Something of a similar situation is suggested by Gray 1969: 'The *mganga* (shaman-diviner), however, has a rival for prestige in the village *mwalimu*, and, in a few villages, the *sheikh*. The *mganga* is generally more prosperous than the *mwalimu* (traditionally a poor man), but the *mwalimu* has moral ascendancy over the *mganga*. There is no doubt that tension exists between these two characters, not necessarily between them as individual personalities, but between the roles they occupy and between the cultural and ideological systems they represent' (p. 186). However, this antithesis does not necessarily exist in all places. Lienhardt, for example, cites examples from the Kilwa and Lamu areas which suggest that people there do not consciously make a very clear distinction between what may be called 'orthodox Islam' and 'local customs' as is done in northern Mafia, and hence even pious Muslims may not condemn the cult of the spirits to the same extent (cf. Lienhardt 1966, 1968).

3. In using the terms shaman and shamanism I am not following Eliade's (1951) definition, with its implied distinction between shamanism and possession, but rather using the terms in Firth's (1959b) and Lewis's (1971) sense—a shaman as a 'master of spirits'.

4. Berreman has noted for the Paharis in India that 'it is largely as the result of the shaman's decision that one family will have to spend hundreds of rupees and weeks of effort in an elaborate ceremony, while another spends only a few hours and gives only a goat in a simple sacrifice' (1964: 59).

5. An early article on spirit possession on the East African coast (Koritschoner 1936) mentions most of these categories of sea spirits, but the author's categories of land spirits are not found on Mafia. Gray's 1969 article on the Segeju gives 'Ruhani' as a synonym for *jinn*.

6. They have many features in common with the *zar* cults in Ethiopia (Messing 1958), Somalia (Lewis 1969), the Sudan (Constantinides 1972), and other parts of Muslim Africa.

7. The mother had been prevented from carrying her children to term, or else the children had died very young. Thus a compact had been made with the spirit which was troubling her that if the child was allowed to grow up, a present would be given to the spirit. Such presents are normally given when the child has passed the critical first two years of its life, and can walk.

8. For example: cow (*ng'ombe* in Swahili) becomes *mkwavi*
   child (*mtoto* in Swahili) becomes *kengeja*
   woman (*mwanamke* in Swahili) becomes *mwanakasi*
   man (*mwanamume* in Swahili) becomes *dume*

9. During the agricultural season people working in the fields of descent group F, which are associated with spirits, are not allowed to wear rubber manufactured sandals; they must either go bare-foot, or else wear sandals of skins, which they make themselves. Similarly, participants in the land spirit dance rituals are bare-foot.

10. Berreman has pointed this out for the Paharis: 'Shamanism affords people who would otherwise spend their lives deferring to others a role in which they hope to acquire not only prestige and economic well-being, but a large measure of influence on the lives of others, and especially on the lives of their caste superiors who otherwise exert authority over them' (ibid. 62).

11. Similarly, Berreman: 'They are often in a position to decide responsibility of guilt in inter-personal difficulties, and then to influence, if not actually decide, the atonement to be made . . .' (ibid. 59).

Chapter 7

1. The same kind of situation exists at the higher levels as well. Despite the existence of three structures, the *Boma* (central government office), the District Council, and TANU, each of which is separately housed in Kilindoni, the Tanzanian government deliberately blurs the distinction between them. Thus the Area Commissioner (formerly called District Commissioner) who is the head of the Boma is also Secretary of the District TANU branch; and in 1967 the two posts of Chairman of TANU and Chairman of the District Council were amalgamated.

2. Compare a very similar situation in a Hindu village in Nepal—Caplan 1972, 1974.

3. In fact, I learned after leaving the field that a Pokomo actually became village Chairman the following year.

4. As she had already been married and divorced, she was considered an adult, and could therefore, in theory, marry whomsoever she pleased. She still needed a male relative, however, to speak for her and settle the bride-payment (*mahari*) and give consent on her behalf at the marriage ceremony which is not normally attended by women, even the bride herself.

Chapter 8

1. cf. Levi-Strauss 1953, Nutini 1965, Ogan 1966.

2. As Ogan rightly points out: 'The model does not utilize any of the theoretical bases of formal statistics . . . (hence) . . . the modest designation "numerical" might be more appropriate' (1966: 180 n.) However, I have retained the term 'statistical' because most anthropologists understand it to mean 'what people do' (cf. Levi-Strauss 1953, Leach 1961, Nutini 1965, Scheffler 1965, Keesing 1967a).

3. Obviously this line of reasoning constitutes something of a tautology; indeed, it is almost a circular argument. However, I would justify its use by pointing out that it is an heuristic device.

BIBLIOGRAPHY

ANDERSON, J. N. D. 1959. 'Waqfs in East Africa'. *Journal of African Law*, vol. 3.

BAILEY, A. P. 1965. *Land Tenure: its Sociological Implications, with Specific Reference to the Swahili-speaking Peoples of the East African Coast.* Thesis presented for the degree of Master of Arts, University of London.

BAUMANN, O. 1896. 'Die Insel Mafia' in *Wissenschaftliche Veröffentlichungen des Vereins für Erkands zu Leipzig.* Verlag von Duncker und Humblot, Leipzig. (A partial translation is available in *Tanganyika Notes and Records*, vol. 46, 1957.)

BERREMAN, G. D. 1964. 'Brahmins and Shamans in Pahari Religion'. *Journal of Asian Studies*, vol. 23.

BLOCH, M. 1971. *Placing the Dead.* Seminar Press: London and New York.

BUJRA, J. M. 1968. *An Anthropological Study of Political Action in a Bajuni Village in Kenya.* Thesis presented for the degree of Doctor of Philosophy, University of London.

1973. *Pumwani: The Politics of Property. A Study of an Urban Renewal Scheme.* Unpublished report on a research project sponsored by the Social Science Research Council.

CAPLAN, A. P. 1969. 'Cognatic Descent Groups on Mafia Island, Tanzania'. *Man* (new series), vol. 4.

1972. *Priests and Cobblers: Social Change in a Hindu Village in Western Nepal.* Chandler: San Francisco.

1974. 'Hierarchy or Stratification? Two Case Studies from Nepal and East Africa' in *The Himalayan Interface*, ed. J. Fisher. Mouton: The Hague.

in the press. 'Girls' Puberty and Boys' Circumcision Rites among the Swahili of Mafia Island'. *Africa.*

CHITTICK, N. 1957 et seq. *Annual Reports of the British Institute of History and Archaeology in East Africa.* The British Academy: London.

1961. *Kisimani Mafia, Excavations at an Islamic Settlement on the East African Coast.* Tanganyika Ministry of Education Antiquities Division. Occasional Paper no. 1. Dar es Salaam.

CONSTANTINIDES, P. 1972. *Sickness and the Spirits: a Study of the Zar Spirit Possession Cult in the Northern Sudan.* Thesis presented for the degree of Doctor of Philosophy, University of London.

ELIADE, M. 1951. *Le chamanisme et les techniques archaïques de l'extase,*

Paris. (English translation *Shamanism.* Routledge and Kegan Paul: London 1964.)

FIRTH, R. 1957. 'A Note on Descent Groups in Polynesia'. *Man,* vol. 57.

1959a. *Social Change in Tikopia.* Allen and Unwin: London.

*1959b. 'Problem and Assumption in an Anthropological Study of Religion'. *J. roy. anthrop. inst.,* vol. 89.

1963. 'Bilateral Descent Groups' in I. Schapera (ed.) *Studies in Kinship and Marriage.* R.A.I. Occasional Paper no. 16. London.

FREEMAN-GRENVILLE, G. S. P. 1962. *The Mediaeval History of the Coast of Tanganyika.* Oxford University Press: London.

GIBB, H. A. R. and KRAMERS, J. H. 1961. *Shorter Encyclopaedia of Islam.* E. J. Brill: Leiden. Luzac and Co: London.

GLUCKMAN, M. 1943. *Lozi Land and Royal Property.* Rhodes-Livingstone Paper no. 10. Manchester University Press: Manchester.

GOODENOUGH, W. H. 1955. 'A Problem in Malayo-Polynesian Social Organisation'. *American Anthropologist,* vol. 67.

GRAY, R. F. 1969. 'The Shetani Cult among the Segeju of Tanzania' in J. Beattie and J. Middleton (eds.) *Spirit Mediumship and Society in Africa.* Routledge and Kegan Paul: London.

GULLIVER, P. H. 1971. *Neighbours and Networks.* University of California Press: Berkeley and Los Angeles.

HANSON, F. A. 1970a. *Rapan Lifeways.* Little, Brown: Boston.

1970b. 'Nonexclusive Cognatic Descent in Rapa' in A. Howard (ed.) *Polynesia: Readings in a Culture Area.* Chandler: San Francisco.

HARRIES, L. 1962. *Swahili Poetry.* Oxford University Press: London.

HOBEN, A. 1973. *Land Tenure among the Amhara of Ethiopia: the Dynamics of Cognatic Descent.* University of Chicago Press: Chicago and London.

KEESING, R. M. 1967a. 'Statistical Models and Decision Models of Social Structure: a Kwaio Case'. *Ethnology,* vol. 6.

1967b. *Kwaio Descent Groups.* Unpublished ms. University of California: Santa Cruz.

1970. 'Shrines, Ancestors and Cognatic Descent: The Kwaio and Tallensi'. *American Anthropologist,* vol. 72.

KING, N. 1917. 'Mafia'. *Geographical Journal,* vol. 50.

KORITSCHONER, H. 1936. 'Ngoma ya Shaitani: an East African Native Treatment for Psychical Disorders'. *J. roy. anthrop. inst.,* vol. 50.

LEACH, E. R. 1961. *Pul Eliya.* Cambridge University Press: Cambridge.

1962. 'A Note on the Mangaian Kopu'. *American Anthropologist,* vol. 64.

LEVI-STRAUSS, C. 1953. 'Social Structure' in A. L. Kroeber (ed.) *Anthropology Today.* University of Chicago Press: Chicago.

LEWIS, I. M. 1966. 'Spirit Possession and Deprivation Cults'. *Man* (new series), vol. 1.

1969. 'Spirit Possession in Northern Somaliland' in J. Beattie and J. Middleton (eds.) *Spirit Mediumship and Society in Africa.* Routledge and Kegan Paul: London.

1970. 'A Structural Approach to Witchcraft and Spirit Possession' in M. Douglas (ed.) *Witchcraft Confessions and Accusations.* ASA Monograph no. 9. Tavistock: London.

1971. *Ecstatic Religion.* Penguin: London.

LIENHARDT, P. 1958. 'The Mosque College of Lamu and its Social Background'. *Tanganyika Notes and Records*. vol. 53.

— 1966. 'A Controversy over Islamic Custom in Kilwa Kivinje, Tanzania' in I. Lewis (ed.) *Islam in Tropical Africa*. Oxford University Press for International African Institute: London.

— 1968. *The Medicine Man*. Oxford University Press: London.

LLOYD, P. C. 1966. 'Agnatic and Cognatic Descent among the Yoruba'. *Man* (new series), vol. 1.

MACGEAGH, W. M. and ADDIS, W. 1945. *Review of Systems of Land Tenure in Zanzibar Protectorate*. Zanzibar.

MAFIA DISTRICT BOOK. Undated. Unpublished collection of mss. in the Area Commissioner's Office, Kilindoni, Mafia.

MAINE, H. 1861. *Ancient Law*. Reprinted 1963. Beacon Press: Boston.

MAYER, A. C. 1966. 'The Significance of Quasi-groups in the Study of Complex Societies' in M. Banton (ed.) *The Social Anthropology of Complex Societies*. ASA Monograph no. 4. Tavistock: London.

MESSING, S. D. 1958. 'Group Therapy and Social Status in the Zar Cult of Ethiopia'. *American Anthropologist*, vol. 60.

MIDDLETON, J. 1961. *Report on Land Tenure in Zanzibar*. Colonial Research Studies, no. 33. HMSO: London.

NUTINI, H. G. 1965. 'Some Considerations on the Nature of Social Structure and Model Building: a Critique of Claude Levi-Strauss and Edmund Leach'. *American Anthropologist*, vol. 67.

OGAN, E. 1966. 'Nasioi Marriage: an Essay in Model-building'. *Southwestern Journal of Anthropology*, vol. 22.

OLIVER, R. and MATHEW, G. 1963. *History of East Africa*. Oxford University Press: London.

PAKENHAM, R. H. W. 1947. *Land Tenure among the Wahadimu at Chwaka, Zanzibar Island*. Zanzibar.

PIGGOTT, D. W. I. 1941. 'History of Mafia'. *Tanganyika Notes and Records*, vols. 11 and 12.

PRINS, A. H. J. 1961. *The Swahili-speaking Peoples of Zanzibar and the East African Coast*. Ethnographic Survey of Africa: East-Central Africa, part 12. International African Institute: London.

RADCLIFFE-BROWN, A. R. and FORDE, D. 1950. *African Systems of Kinship and Marriage*. Oxford University Press for International African Institute: London.

REVINGTON, T. M. 1936. 'Notes on the Mafia Island Group'. *Tanganyika Notes and Records*, vol. 1.

SCHEFFLER, H. W. 1965. *Choiseul Island Social Structure*. University of California Press: Berkeley and Los Angeles.

— 1966. 'Ancestor Worship in Anthropology; or, Observations on Descent and Descent Groups'. *Current Anthropology*, vol. 7.

TANGANYIKA. 1958. *Population Census 1957*. Nairobi.
Report on the Non-African Census 1957. Dar es Salaam.

TANZANIA, 1969. *United Republic of Tanzania Population Census for 1967*. Central Statistical Bureau: Dar es Salaam.

TANNER, R. E. S. 1958a. 'Fertility and Child Mortality in Cousin Marriage'. *Eugenics Review*, vol. 49.

158   BIBLIOGRAPHY

1958b. 'Small Holdings on the Tanga Coast'. *East African Agricultural Journal*, vol. 24.

1959. *The Social and Kinship System of Pangani District, Tanganyika Territory, 1955–8*. Thesis presented for the degree of B.Litt. University of Oxford.

1960. 'Land Rights on the Tanganyika Coast'. *African Studies*, vol. 19.

1962. 'The Relationships between the Sexes in a Coastal Islamic Community'. *African Studies*, vol. 21.

1964. 'Cousin Marriage in Mombasa'. *Africa*, vol. 34.

TRIMINGHAM, J. 1964. *Islam in East Africa*. Oxford University Press: London.

WEBER, M. 1965. *Theory of Social and Economic Organisation* (part 1 of *Wirtschaft und Gesellschaft*), trans. A. M. Henderson and T. Parsons. New York and London.

WIJEYEWARDENE, G. 1961. *Some Aspects of Village Solidarity among Kiswahili-speaking Communities of Kenya and Tanganyika*. Thesis presented for the degree of Doctor of Philosophy, University of Cambridge.

WILSON, P. 1967. 'Status Ambiguity and Spirit Possession'. *Man* (new series), vol. 2.

INDEX

administration, village, 124–5
adultery, 132
affines, 19, 34, 38, 43, 81
agriculture, 9–10, 59, 77, 119 n.
Amhara, xvii
ancestors, 20, 22, 28, 38, 53, 72, 90, 106
Arabic, Arabs, 2, 3, 4, 5, 8, 14, 32, 33 n., 85, 86, 87, 88, 90, 91, 92, 100, 101, 113, 119, 126; élite, 4, 85, 119–20
astrology, 15, 113, 115

Bailey, A. P., 22 n.
Bajuni, see Gunya
Baumann, O., 21, 23
beans, 10, 14, 59
Berreman, G. D., 108 n., 122 n., 123 n.
birth, 33 n., 89, 113, 115, 117–18, 121
Bujra, J. M., 85, 87
burial, 53

cashew nuts, xv, 5, 11 n., 75 n.
cassava, 9, 10, 41, 59
cattle, 5, 9, 12–13, 17, 90, 109, 120
children, 5, 9, 17, 20, 31, 35, 48, 53, 54, 57, 90, 91, 102, 103, 106, 111, 113, 117–18, 121, 136; fostering of, 49, 50, 51
Christians, 4
circumcision, 26, 89
cloves, xv, 2
coconut trees, 1, 2, 4, 5, 6, 11–12, 17, 39, 52, 53, 55, 57, 74, 75, 76, 78, 87; compulsory planting, 5, 21; groves, 28; inheritance, 29, 41, 43; means of acquiring, 41–2, 45; ownership, 40; plantations, 2, 4, 5, 39; price, 7; renting, 44; residence and, 46; sale of, 42–3
cooking groups, 21–2

co-operatives, 11, 17, 131–3, 136, 137, 140
copra, xv, 5, 11, 13, 15, 18, 75 n., 131, 132
corn, 10, 59
councils, 17, 28, 124, 127, 128
crafts, 16–17
crops, 39, 41, 59, 60, 77; cash, 5, 6, 9, 10, 11
courts, 71, 75, 124, 125
curses, 106

dances, dancing, 35, 89, 109, 119, 123
Dar es Salaam, 6, 13, 14, 16, 126, 128, 131, 132, 136
death, 90, 106, 109, 113
descent groups (*vikao*), xvi–xix, 19–38; functions, 20, 21, 22; guilds, 105, 114–15, 116; Islam, 84, 85, 94–9; land, 39–40, 43, 58–61, 68, 78; membership, 19–20, 24, 31–2; office holders, 127–8, 129, 137–49 *passim*; residence, 47, 78–83; segments, 22, 23, 35, 36, 39, 52, 63, 65–69 *passim*, 96; size, 29, 30; spirit possession, 100, 103, 109, 123; structure, 19
diet, 10, 11, 34
disputes, 28, 29, 53, 125; land, 65–75; of sheikhs, 94–6
District Agricultural Officer, 59, 60
diviners, divination, 15, 103, 104, 107, 108, 109, 117
Divisional Executive Officer, 124, 127
divorce, 27, 29, 31, 44, 50, 52, 57, 75, 117, 132, 139
donkeys, 6, 13
dress, 4, 130

ear-piercing, 89
education, 5, 88, 90; see schools